DER GEIST Volume 3 Number 1, Issue 3

Copyright © 2020 Trevor Blake and Kevin I. Slaughter. All Rights Reserved.

Editor: Trevor Blake
Co-Editor and Designer: Kevin I. Slaughter
Copy Editors: Anonymous, Fred Woodworth

First Printing: February, 2020
[Stirner, Max]; Blake, Trevor; Slaughter, Kevin I.
ISBN 978-1-944651-16-9
ISSN 2639-5339
Philosophy
Reference

SUBSCRIPTIONS are not available at press time.
BULK RATES and DISTRIBUTORS and INSTITUTIONS please inquire.

UNIONOFEGOISTS.COM

UoE West Coast

Der Geist, Inquiries & Reviews
LETTERS:
    Trevor Blake
    P. O. Box 2321
    Portland, OR 97208-2321
    UNITED STATES
PACKAGES:
    Trevor Blake
    715 NW Hoyt Street #2321
    Portland, OR 97208-2321
    UNITED STATES

UoE East Coast

UnionOfEgoists.com, *Stand Alone*
LETTERS & PACKAGES:
    Union of Egoists
    444 Maryland Ave #7940
    Essex, MD 21221
    UNITED STATES
EMAIL:
    editor@unionofegoists.com

Not responsible for unsolicited materials.

INTRODUCTION

Welcome to the third issue of *Der Geist*, published by the Union of Egoists. The Union of Egoists publishes rare reprints and original inquiries into the philosophy of egoism as published between 1845 and 1945. Egoism begins in 1845 with the publication of *Der Einzige und sein Eigentum* (*The Ego and His Own*) by Max Stirner. Egoism does not end one hundred years later, but the year 1945 provides a poetic and practical punctuation point for our publishing. *Der Geist* is not an advocate of any course of action.[1] *Der Geist* may aid in the study of egoism, but it is not a journal advocating for or against egoism. Readers may find our work builds up or tears down egoism, but our scholarship is impeccable. Make of it what you will.

This issue of *Der Geist* includes rare reprints of egoist history. These include blow-by-blow accounts of Dora Marsden in her street-fighting phase, lost transcriptions of J. William Lloyd saved from the darkness by individualist feminist Wendy McElroy, the philosophical and physical wanderings of the laughing philosopher Malfew Seklew, and more. This issue of *Der Geist* also includes original inquiries into egoist history. These include a history of the Radical Book Shop of Chicago, and the heretofore undocumented bands of iron that link the Industrial Workers of the World (the "Wobblys") and Ragnar Redbeard's book *Might is Right*.

Our critics continue apace, as they have from our advent. Where would we be without our Muslim stalkers and busybodies? One particularly inspired *jihadi* immolated himself in December 2018, to which we give a slow and metered round of applause. Another altruistic agent of Allah produced pirate printings of our periodicals. He could have simply done so and neither explained nor apologized, therefore demonstrating an understanding of egoism. Instead, he did it for 'freedom' or 'liberty' or *'dar al-Islam'* or some other imaginary friend from whom he seeks approval. Tsk tsk.

As if *Der Geist* were not sufficient to engage every egoist for aeons, your editors have also published significant new editions of important individualist books since the previous issue. Underworld Amusements has published *Might is Right: The Authoritative Edition* by Ragnar Redbeard. This edition harmonizes the complete text of

---

1   With the exception being a hearty cheer for those who buy our publications.

every edition of *Might is Right* published in the author's lifetime, and then adds literally thousands of annotations to give the broad-axe swing of this book both weight and distance. The Union of Egoists has published *A Brave and Beautiful Spirit: Dora Marsden (1882 – 1960)* by Dr. Les Garner. *A Brave and Beautiful Spirit* has been out of print since 1990. Used copies regularly appeared for hundreds of dollars in the trade. This new and eminently affordable edition includes many illustrations, additions, corrections, a new Foreword and a greatly expanded index. For more information on these books, and on all of our work, please regularly consult UnionOfEgoists.com

> —Trevor Blake
> editor, *Der Geist*
> Kevin I. Slaughter
> editor, UnionOfEgoists.com

STAND ALONE

Egoist and related mixed-format companion to *Der Geist*. Published continuously since 2016. From books to t-shirts to podcasts and everything in-between. For more information see:

unionofegoists.com/journals/stand-alone-2016/

DORA MARSDEN

In 1908 Dora joined and became a leader in the Women's Social and Political Union (WSPU). The following year she resigned as a teacher and became a full-time agitator for the WSPU. She was sentenced to two months in prison for vandalism in 1909. After a hunger strike she was released and continued to agitate and disrupt political meetings (including a speech by a young Winston Churchill).

In 1911, Dora founded *The Freewoman* (1911–1912). Financial troubles led to a re-launch as *The New Freewoman* (1914). An ever-more keen search for liberty led to a re-launch as *The Egoist* (1914–1919).

In the 1920s–1930s Dora wrote three books: *The Definition of the Godhead* (1928), *The Mysteries of Christianity* (1930) and *The Philosophy of Time* (published in 1955). During the writing of these books she went from a self-imposed isolation to confinement in a mental hospital, where she spent the remainder of her life.

> There is only one person concerned in the freeing of individuals: and that is the person who wears and feels and resents the shackles. Shackles must be burst off: if they are cut away from outside, they will immediately reform.
> —Dora Marsden, *The Freewoman* Vol. 1 No. 1 (June 15 1913)

Dora Marsden under arrest 1909.

Brave and Beautiful 7
Trevor Blake (2019)

Dora Marsden, Hatless and Disheveled. 9
(uncredited) (1900)
Two accounts from March 31st, 1900 of a street-fighting egoist. The first an excerpt from the *Nottingham Evening Post* and the second the *Manchester Courier and Lancashire General Advertiser*. For all the blood and thunder of most egoist authors, only a few are known to have committed acts of physical violence. Those few include the Bonnot Gang and Dora Marsden. This street battle took place during Dora's time with the Women's Social and Political Union (WSPU), an organization she later left as limiting her liberty. After the WSPU she founded *The Freewoman*, later *The New Freewoman*, later *The Egoist*, magazines where she moved from votes for women, to freedom for men and women, to freedom from freedom, to freedom from time and space and language. Some of those arrested with Dora on this day were later writers and editors for her magazines.

Introduction to "The Next Advance…" 17
Trevor Blake (2019)

The Freewoman—the Next Advance in the Progress of Feminism . 20
Conservative and Unionist Women's Franchise Review (1912)

The Malthusian League 23
Trevor Blake (2019)

An Event of Considerable Importance. 25
The Malthusian League (1912)
"An Event of Considerable Importance" appeared in *The Thirty-Fourth Annual Report of the Malthusian League* (London: William Bell 1912).

Introduction to "A New Prophetess of Feminism" 27
Trevor Blake (2019)

A New Prophetess of Feminism 28
Frances Maule Bjorkman (1912)

Brave and Beautiful
Trevor Blake (2019)

> One point at least in our "attitude" has been caught - our "commonness." It is cardinal, and we must insist on it. We are "common." This does not mean, either on our lips, or on others, that we are like everybody else. *Tout au contraire!* It means that we are egoistic, individual, selfish. To be "common" with the "fine" means to be in the bonds of selfish motives and to see others in the same - not to be under sway of the fine concepts; the "noble" emotions; to be running amok of the whole cultural structure. And so we are. We are seeking our individual satisfactions, and find instruction in tracing out the ridiculous figure cut by those who are gadding about pretending to seek other peoples.
> —*The Freewoman*, Volume 1 Number 2, July 1st 1913

In our first issue we published a new biographical sketch of the life and thoughts of Dora Marsden. In our second issue we published an original map of her London, including the location of the Freewomen Discussion Circle, the first union of egoists. Then, as now, we accompany our research with reprinted essays and rare images of the publisher of *The Freewoman*, *The New Freewoman* and *The Egoist*.

In this the third issue of *Der Geist* we are pleased to announce the publication of a new edition of *A Brave and Beautiful Spirit: Dora Marsden (1882–196)* by Les Garner. This is the only biography of Dora Marsden to be published. *Brave and Beautiful* is written from the author's perspective as a socialist and a feminist, and Dr. Garner does not shy away from spirited criticism of egoism as found in the works of Max Stirner and Dora Marsden. The book has been out of print since 1990, and the rare copy that appears on the secondary market usually exceeds four hundred US dollars. This new edition from the Union of Egoists is newly revised, expanded and corrected, with a new forward from the author and a new index by Trevor Blake. Available worldwide, see UnionOfEgoists.com for details.

Dora Marsden, Hatless and Disheveled
(Uncredited) (1900)

Nottingham Evening Post March 31st, 1900

INCIDENTS OF THE RAID
DISAPPOINTED SUFFRAGISTS
ONLY ONE OF THEM ADMITTED TO THE HOUSE
TWELVE ARRESTS

In accordance with the statement contained in Miss Pankhurst's letter to the Prime Minister on Monday, the members of the Women's Social and Political Union assembled in large numbers at Caxton Hall yesterday afternoon for the purpose of appointing a deputation to wait upon Mr. Asquith at the House of Commons.

Compared with previous gatherings of a similar nature, there was less enthusiasm in the proceedings, while in the streets there were further evidences of declining interest in the propaganda methods of the Union. A brass band aided in engendering a bellicose spirit by playing patriotic marches before the meeting.

The usual resolution, calling upon the Government to abandon their present policy and to give votes to those women disqualified by sex, was proposed by Mrs. Solomon, seconded by Mrs. Eates, and supported by Miss Smith (Birmingham), Mrs. Morris (Liverpool), Miss Woodlock (Liverpool), Miss Robinson (Manchester), and Miss Dora Marsden (Manchester).

The deputation, 29 in number, left Caxton Hall at ten minutes to four to the strains of the Marseillaise played by the band, and the encouraging cheers of a number of women sympathisers. Miss Dora Marsden carried the suffragist tricolour at the head of the procession. The deputation had only gone about fifty yards when the police stopped it, and courteously explained that their formation constituted a procession, which could not be allowed within a mile of the House. Miss Marsden was allowed to pass the cordon leaning on the arm of a gentleman, and still carrying her tricolour. Other members of the party were passed through one at a time, and at such intervals as to render a procession out of the question. Miss Marsden reached the St. Stephen's entrance just after four o'clock, and, of course, did not get beyond the police who guarded the entrance.

POLICE CAPTURE THE COLOURS

An exciting half-hour followed. Miss Marsden insisted on carrying her colours aloft, and the police broke the pole so as to prevent her doing this. She, however, retained the remains of her flag, and made determined attempts to mount the steps leading to the House of Commons. Altogether about twenty-four members of the deputation had now reached St. Stephen's, where they were met by a solid cordon of police, and effectively prevented in their endeavours to gain admittance.

Acting Superintendent Boxall had given instructions that nobody should be arrested if arrests could possibly be avoided, and in carrying out that instruction his men displayed the utmost good temper and forbearance. Again and again the women secured a foothold on the pavement, and as they refused to return to the roadway they were pushed off as gently as might be. Some women insisted on addressing the crowd, but appeared to have few sympathisers in the gathering. There was good deal of chaff, and the women were repeatedly advised to "go home."

Two or three mounted policemen helped to keep the crowd on the move, and some of the more daring of the women contrived to seize the bridles of the horses, and were forced away with the greatest difficulty.

The police had absolute control, as was shown by the fact that they readily made a way to the House for a number of ladies who had legitimate business there, and for members passing to and from the House.

The Earl of Granard and his bride presented themselves, and surveyed for some time the exciting scene with evident amusement. The Earl ultimately passed into the House, and the Countess remained in her motor car and ordered it back home.

POLICEMEN'S FACES SMACKED

Shortly before five o'clock the police were compelled, in spite of their desire to avoid arrests, to take a small party of women to Cannon-row Police-station. The offenses alleged against them are of assault against the police. One woman deliberately struck a constable over the head with her umbrella, knocking his helmet off, and twice slapped the officer's face. A second woman who was taken into custody also knocked off a policeman's helmet. The leader and bearer of the bannerette became very violent, and, hatless and disheveled, again and again threw herself against the police cordon. Supt. Wells caught her in his arms as she made the rush and turned her back. The woman tried to strike him in the face, but Mr. Wells would not hear of her being arrested. One of his inspectors was also struck in the face, but showed similar forbearance.

In all the police made twelve arrests, the prisoners being:

- Mrs. Emily Davidson, 4, Clement's Inn, London
- Miss Patricia Woodlock, Canning-chambers, Liverpool
- Mrs. Florence Farmer, 156, Tufnell Park-road, London
- Miss Helen Tolson, Zealand Hall, Manchester
- Miss Margaret Smith, 11, Colore-buildings, Birmingham
- Miss Dora Marsden, Manchester
- Miss Kate Noblet, 63, Bristol-road, Edgbaston
- Miss Alice Burton, 15, Upper Newington, LIverpool
- Mrs. Julia Scott, Woodfield, St. Anne-road, Chertsey
- Mrs. Bessie K. Morris, Wavertree
- Miss Rona Robinson, Fallowfield
- Mr. William Hutcheon, 113, Pepya-road, London, S. E.

Manchester Courier and Lancashire General Advertiser
March 31st, 1900

IN FRONT OF THE PARTY WAS MISS DORA MARSDEN
DESPERATE SUFFRAGETTES.
RAID ON THE COMMONS.
LANCASHIRE LADIES ARRESTED.

Members the National Women's Social and Political Union assembled in large numbers at a "Parliament for Women" at Caxton Hall, Westminster, yesterday, in readiness for another attempt to interview the Prime Minister on the question of women's suffrage. Mrs.

Pankhurst presided over the "Parliament," and was supported on the platform by Miss Christabel Pankhurst and the members the deputation, all of whom wore "Votes for Women" sashes and carried a copy of the resolution folded up and tied with purple, green and white ribbon—the colours of the union.

A resolution was passed demanding votes for women, and appointing a deputation to carry a copy of it to the Prime Minister at the House of Commons, and to elicit his reply. Amid applause the following ladies selected for the deputation formed in procession and left for the House:

Representing London: Mrs. Saul Solomon, who was a member of the last deputation and led the procession. Mrs. Eates, Mrs. Birnstingh, Mrs. Reinold, Mrs. S. M. Watson, Mrs. Florence Farmer, Miss Dora Smart, Miss D'Elsa, Miss Kathleen Streatfield, Miss Norah Binnie, Miss Florence Peek, Miss Louise Till, Mrs. Julia Scott, and Mrs. Emily Walding-Davidson.

Birmingham: Miss Kate Noblet and Miss Margaret Smith.

Manchester: Miss Helen Tolson, Miss Pepper, Miss Sanders, Miss Ethel Cockburn, Miss Dora Marsden, Miss Robinson, and Mrs. Mary Wiseman.

Liverpool: Mies Patricia Woodlock, Miss Broughton, Mrs. Bessie K. Morris, Miss Alice Burton, and Mrs. Hilton.

Lancaster: Miss Selina Martin.

MARCH TO THE HOUSE.

As the ladies emerged from the hall a band played the "Marseillaise," and the crowded gathering cheered loudly. In front of the party was Miss Dora Marsden, carrying the Union colours. They marched slowly in along compact formation till they arrived at the end of the street, where they were met by an inspector at the head of a body of policemen and stopped. There was a little parleying, and somehow Miss Dora Marsden, the colour bearer, wriggled through and went marching boldly along Victoria street, holding her purple, white, and green banner aloft. Presently Miss Farmer and Miss Scott also got through the cordon as the procession was broken up, and marched side by side with Miss Marsden, with whom Mr. Holland Birch was walking. There was a drizzling rain. As they proceeded along the street the three ladies were continually separated, but came together again.

At Parliament square a detachment of mounted police rode up, and as Miss Marsden persisted her efforts get through she became rather dangerously mixed up with three horses, and the pole of her banner was snapped. Amid a scene of some excitement the ladies were forced back, when was discovered that other members the deputation had got round by another route and were marching on to St. Stephen's entrance. An excited rush of people took place, but the ladies reached the entrance, and there found the hall blocked by policemen, with a large number of members of Parliament standing on the steps inside.

STATE OF SIEGE.

The leader of the women asked to see the Prime Minister and, failing him, Colonel Seely. Superintendent Wells, who was charge of the police, told them they could not do so, and they were pushed away. For some considerable time the entrance was in state of siege. The police did not make any arrests, but continually advanced in solid line and pushed the aggressors off the pavement in dangerous proximity to a number of mounted police who were holding the crowd back. Every now and then a single member of the deputation would wriggle round and rush between the arms of the police on the steps. In the scurry the ladies lost their hats and presented bedraggled appearance. Shrieks were heard as they got in dangerous positions near the horses, and some laughter was caused by cries of "Mind your toes, girls."

IN THE HOUSE OF COMMONS.

Mrs. Solomon, the leader of the deputation and a Cape Colony lady, was admitted into the House. Narrating her experiences, she said she was stopped by a cordon of the police, but by means of a friend who was also in the Lobby, she came in the Speaker's entrance. She asked to see Mr. Asquith, but was told he was not in the House. She then asked to see Colonel Seely, whom she knew personally, and subsequently had an interview with him. He was very nice, and said he would be very happy do to anything in his power, but could not carry a message to the Cabinet Minister. The lady remained in the Lobby for some time, and among others sent in her card to Mr. Birrell, stating that she knew a relative of his.

LETTER TO THE PREMIER.

Before leaving the Houses of Parliament Mrs. Solomon, writing on House of Commons notepaper, addressed the following letter to the Premier: "Dear sir,—I have the honour to address you in writing, because I learn that you are not at present in the House. I therefore am unable to have the privilege of seeing you. May I therefore enclose the resolution which I was deputed to lay before you by the Women's Parliament Caxton Hall, and to request that you will give the same earnest consideration." After leaving the building Mrs. Solomon returned to the Hall, and narrated her achievement amid great enthusiasm.

LORD CROMER'S EXPERIENCE.

The proceedings outside were watched by several members of the House of Lords, including the Primate and the Bishop of Southwark. The police performed their tasks with commendable good humour. Instructions had been given them to make no arrests except in the case of violence on the part of the Suffragettes. Miss Lonsdale attempted to harangue the crowd by means of a megaphone. She was uninterrupted for few moments, but then the police closed on her, the megaphone was wrested from her grasp, and she was hurried away. As Lord Cromer's private motor car drove up a Suffragette wrenched the further door open and leapt into the car amid terrific cheers from the crowd. She shut the door, the police forced it open and hauled her out. Acting under the direction of the police, the chauffeur, in the excitement of the moment, drove off, leaving Lord Cromer standing on the pavement. Eventually a way was made for him through the mob, and he was enabled to enter the car and drive away.

STRUCK A CONSTABLE.

At last the Suffragettes got out of hand, and arrests were made. Two of the women from Lancashire made a determined rush at the main gate of Palace Yard, and one of the women, striking a constable in the face, was arrested. In the thick of the riot Miss Christabel Pankhurst drove through the crowd in a cab. Three other ladies created diversion by driving up to the St. Stephen's entrance in a hansom. As they alighted one of them was seen to take some banners from the seat, when the police rushed and told the cabman to drive away. The ladies got out a short distance off and were returning, but a mounted policeman rode behind the one bearing the banners and cleverly snatched them out of her hand, broke the staves, and handed them to a cyclist policeman.

LADIES ARRESTED.

The names of the arrested are:

- Emily Davison, teacher, 4, Clement's Inn, assault.
- Patricia Woodlock, 2, South John-street, Liverpool, obstruction.
- Mrs. Florence Farmer, Clement's Inn, obstruction.
- Ellen Tolson, Hall, Cheshire, obstruction.
- Emily Margaret Anne Smith, 11, Buildings, Henrietta-street, Birmingham, obstruction.
- Dora Marsden, 141, Charlton-road, Manchester, obstruction and assault.
- Julia Scott, 4, Clement's Inn, obstruction.
- Messie Morris, 2, Overton-street, Edge Hill, Liverpool, assault.
- Rona Robinson, Brinslea Villas, Brook-road, Fallowfield, Manchester, obstruction and assault.
- William Hutcheon, 113, Pepys-road, Wimbledon, journalist, obstruction.
- Kate Nobletts 86, Bristol-road, Birmingham, obstruction and assault.
- Alice Eliza Burton, 15, Upper Newington, Liverpool, obstruction.

They will be brought this morning, probably at Bow-street Police Court.

ANOTHER DEPUTATION.

It was announced last night at the offices of the Women's Social and Political Union that those members the deputation who had not been arrested will visit the House of Commons tomorrow afternoon with the object of obtaining an interview with the Prime Minister. Mr. Asquith has been notified to this effect.

PROTECTING THE CABINET.

Mr. Asquith presided over a meeting of the Cabinet yesterday morning. The police, in view of the programme of the Suffragists, sent special force to Downing-street to intercept any deputation which might seek to reach the Prime Minister at his official residence, but no Suffragists appeared on the scene.

MISS PANKHURT'S OPPORTUNITY.

Mr. Winston Churchill, M.P., Lord Robert Cecil. M.P.. and Miss Pankhurst will be the principal guests at the annual dinner of the West London "Parliament."

Introduction to "The Next Advance in the Progress of Feminism"
Trevor Blake (2019)

What follows is an early review of *The Freewoman* by Dora Marsden and Mary Gawthorpe from *The Conservative and Unionist Women's Franchise Review* for January 1st, 1912. The review appeared in the newspaper of the Conservative and Unionist Women's Franchise Association (circa 1908 - 1918). This organization was met as part of the National Union of Women's Suffrage Societies:

> to form a bond of union between all Conservatives and Unionists who are in favour of the removal of the sex disqualification, and the extension of the franchise to all duly qualified women; to convince members of the Conservative and Unionist Party of the desirability of this policy, and as far as is possible to give active support to official candidates at elections when they are in favour of the enfranchisement of women; to work for women's enfranchisement by educative and constitutional methods consistent with Unionist principles.[1]

The review lists the "Contents of First Number." This largely but not exactly matches the Table of Contents for *The Freewoman* Volume 1 Number 1. The items are not listed in the order they are published. Some items as published are described slightly differently in the review. The Table of Contents lists "Der Bund für Mutterschutz" with a subtitle "A German League for the Protection of Mothers" while the review lists "A German League for the Protection of Women." "The Fashioning of Florence Isabel" is described in the review as "Short Story." "A University Degree for Housewives?" is described in the review as "University Degree for Housewives." The review was published on January 1st, 1912, and *The Freewoman* was published on November 23rd, 1911. The small differences between the "Contents

---

1   "Woman's Suffrage" in *Hazell's Annual* Volume 26 (1911) page 397

of First Number" and *The Freewoman* as published suggest the author of the review saw a manuscript of the first issue of *The Freewoman* prior to its publication. This review, therefore, is a glimpse into the process of creating *The Freewoman* - "the next advance in the progress of Feminism."

Stephen Swift was the publishing firm for *The Freewoman*, and Charles Grenville was the owner of Stephen Swift. Grenville was an enthusiastic supporter of *The Freewoman* and served as the chair for the Freewoman Discussion Circle in London. Dora's demands upon his support increased in proportion to her lack of appreciation for a man willing to print her magazines anew at his own expense when she edited them after the fact. When Grenville withdrew his financial support, *The Freewoman* collapsed. Dora repeated the process with the backers for *The New Freewoman*. Once relieved of editorial duties, her third magazine *The Egoist* was able to endure.

The specter of communism reduces all human interactions to struggles for power. When communism came to haunt feminism, feminism came to be about power of enfranchisement and the power of employment and the power of education. But there was no particular reason it needed to turn out that way. Feminism could have been a spiritual or religious movement. The pagan dance of Isadora Duncan, the Theosophy of Helena Blavatsky, the witchcraft of Gerald Gardner, this could have been feminism. Feminism could have been a school of art. Not the feminist art movement that began in the 1970s, but feminism as a school of art from the start. Feminism could have been a movement for individuals. Feminism could have been a branch of science, à la Margaret Sanger or the Malthusian League. Dora Marsden described what she had in mind by way of contrast, describing the opposite of a Freewoman in her essay "The Bondwoman."

> Bondwomen are distinguished from Freewomen by a spiritual distinction. Bondwomen are the women who are not separate spiritual entities who are not individuals. They are complements merely. By habit of thought, by form of activity, and largely by preference, they round off the personality of some other individual, rather than create or cultivate their own. Most women, as far back as we have any record, have fitted into this conception, and it has borne itself out in in-

stinctive working practice. And in the midst of all this there comes a cry that woman is an individual, and that because she is an individual she must be set free. It would be nearer the truth to say that if she is an individual she is free, and will act like those who are free.

While feminism was made dull by mere communism, in this review from The Conservative and Unionist Women's Franchise there remained hope that Feminism could offer something to individuals as individuals.

THE FREEWOMAN—THE NEXT ADVANCE IN THE PROGRESS OF FEMINISM
CONSERVATIVE AND UNIONIST WOMEN'S FRANCHISE REVIEW (1912)

On Thursday, November the twenty-third, 1911, Messrs. Stephen Swift and Co. commenced publication of a new weekly Feminist review, *The Freewoman*, which is under the joint editorship of Miss Dora Marsden and Miss Mary Gawthorpe.

The new undertaking was entered upon in the hope that it will afford the conditions most favourable to a full and frank discussion of Feminism in all its aspects.

The editorial attitude will be taken upon the assumption that Feminism has as yet no definite creed, and that even in respect of what would be regarded as its fundamental proposition, the subject still bristles with interrogations.

It is considered that while the articulate consciousness of mind in women, which in its different forms of expression is called Feminism, is one of the most unmistakable features of modern times, yet, none the less, the readjustments in politics and morals which the new feature will make necessary, form highly debatable questions upon which we have hardly yet entered.

In such circumstances therefore, it has seemed that the next advance in the progress of Feminism would be made through the encouragement of full and open discussion, and it is this encouragement which the new journal will provide.

Literary contributions bearing on the subject will be sought, and all contributions which carry with them quality of thought will be considered, irrespective of their point of view, conventional and otherwise.

The policy of the paper towards the political enfranchisement of women will be to regard it as a subject which has passed out of the sphere of philosophical debate, its enactment into law being acknowledged as inevitable, sooner or later by the politicians, friendly and unfriendly alike. The position occupied by the question is wholly different from that which it occupied at the time it was championed by men like John Stuart Mill. The energy of the new Feminist impulse carried this phase of the movement into a favoured position at the outset, and its accomplishments will now be brought about by a political manouvering, and not by philosophical debate.

The vast important work of women's industrial organisation stands in the same established position.

The theory of economic independence of women is on more debatable ground. The complete application of the theory would involve changes so enormous in the affairs of the community, the family, and the individual that there is doubt and hesitancy as to the manner and extent of its application to be found in the most forward feminist ranks themselves.

An effort will be made to treat the subject of sex morality in a spirit free from bias. Holding the view that conventional sex morality is open to question, the entire subject will be dealt with in an unreservedly fair and straightforward way.

It is believed that Feminism would be conceived in truer perspective if the English movement could keep in review the forms of activity in which the impulse finds expression in countries other than our own It seems undeniable that there has been much of the purely accidental in the forces which have made the movement in England so largely political, and a wider survey would give it a truer significance, and to secure this wider survey, correspondents abroad are being secured.

In so far, however, as the English movement is political, it is necessary that it should find its bearings in modern political thought. In this respect it has a two-fold task. Inasmuch as it does not fall into line with popular democracy, in a democratic community it remains suspect; and, inasmuch as it falls into line, it has to find its defence against the criticisms which are attacking popular democracy itself; especially the latter, as the immediate practical application of feminist ideals would bring to democracy a preponderating volume of its supposed dangers and difficulties.

An attempt will be made to sustain from a feminist standpoint critical reviews of the Drama and of General Literature. It is felt that women have been almost exclusively readers and portrayers and very rarely critics. The vast implications regarding moral sex values which are contained in Literature exert an influence so pervasive that there can be little change in moral estimates as long as such implied standards remain unquestioned.

Literary contributions will be sought from men equally with women, and it is hoped that the paper will find men readers as readily as women. It is considered that any theory of Feminism which regards itself as the private province of women's interests is an absurdity, and that any reputable theory must hold that the interests of men are involved at least equally with those of women.

It is submitted that the enterprise is courageously conceived, and that every effort will be made to carry it out efficiently. It is therefore in a spirit of entire confidence that support is sought from those of the community for whom the subject has an interest.

Introduction to The Malthusian League
Trevor Blake (2019)

Mrs. Havelock Ellis spoke on "Some Problems of Eugenics" in a Freewoman Discussion Circle. The Discussion Circles were the first public individualist organization in the world, beginning its orbit of Dora's magazine *The Freewoman* in February 1912. Dora was likely at that Discussion Circle lecture, but we do not know Dora's views on eugenics. We know that Dora Marsden never had any children, but why she never had children will forever remain speculation. What Dora might have thought of the support of The Malthusian League is also speculation. We can only know that she had their support.

The Malthusian League existed from 1877 to 1927. They attributed poverty not to class conflict but to overpopulation, and therefore advocated not socialism but birth control. "Overpopulation is the most fruitful source of pauperism, ignorance, crime and disease... the full and open discussion of the population question in all its necessary aspects is a matter of vital moment in society." They encouraged "the elimination of unfitness [...] not by restriction of marriage, segregation, or by sterilisation (which should be resorted to only in the case of those obviously incapable of self-control, such as lunatics and criminals), but by the inculcation of the great responsibility of parenthood and of the effects of such hereditary transmission, combined with a general knowledge of the most hygenic means of limiting families."

The leader of The Malthusian League in 1912 was Dr. Alice Vickery. Dr. Vickery was an advocate of birth control at a time when even public discussion of birth control was illegal. She also advocated a reduction in the stigma associated with illegitimacy, and in that she shared a symbolic stage with Leighton Pagan, author of *For Love and Money*. Mary Gawthorpe (1881 - 1973) was a suffragette beaten by police and torture-fed in prison, leading to a lifetime of health problems. She later gave her support to the Campaign for Nuclear Disarmament. After *The Egoist*, Grace Jardine opened a bookstore in Manchester England. Her bookstore sold four copies of Dora's book *The Definition of the Godhead* (London: Egoist Press 1928), representing four of the six copies that sold in Dora's lifetime. Dr. Charles Vickery Drysdale (1874 - 1961) was a later President of The Malthusian League, was founder of the British Men's League for Women's Suffrage, and (entirely outside his area of expertise) was the inventor of the phase-shift transformer. Dr. Drysdale was the author of *Can Everybody Be Fed? / A Reply to Prince Kropotkin* (London: George Standing 1892). Upton Sinclair (1878 - 1968) wrote against exploitive labor in *The Jungle* (1906), against yellow journalism in *The Brass Check* (1919), and against anti-Semitism in *The Flivver King* (1937).

Ecclesiastical advisors have supported sanctions against the spread of information about eugenics / family planning, sexually transmitted diseases and prostitution. Dora's magazines were disallowed by some distributors on these grounds. Altruists will always advise what is advantageous to all. Only amoral and selfish egoists publish citation-rich works and allow the reader to work it out as an individual.

AN EVENT OF CONSIDERABLE IMPORTANCE
THE MALTHUSIAN LEAGUE (1912)

An event of considerable importance during the year has been the advent of the new feminist newspaper: *The Freewoman*, under the leadership of Miss Dora Marsden and Miss Mary Gawthorpe, ably seconded by Miss Grace Jardine. This paper made its first appearance on November 23rd, 1911, and it has throughout been characterized by the most remarkable openness of mind and expression, no subject whatever seeming to have been banned. A series of articles on the population question from the feminist and economic standpoints were contributed by Dr. Drysdale [Volume 1 Number 2, November 30th, 1911], and produced the most animated discussion, in which a fair measure of agreement was shown with neo-Malthusian doctrines. Among the opponents it was interesting to note that some granted the laws of Malthus but objected to preventive means, while others advocated prevention for individual reasons and strongly challenged the population doctrine. It is greatly to be regretted that many Socialists still seem determined to heap ridicule and abuse upon the Malthusian doctrine, and their controversial methods make it impossible for any self-respecting person to argue with them. It is their refusal to recognize this doctrine which has hampered their own efforts, and the new Syndicalist movement appears to show that State Socialism is breaking down just as it appeared to be winning.

Mr. Fliigel [?] contributed two interesting letters to the discussion, upholding the neo-Malthusian side; and an interesting feature was the declaration by Mr. Upton Sinclair, in the issue of January 18 [Volume 1 Number 9, 1912], in which he warmly advocated family limitation and said, *inter alia*:

> This new discovery of science gives us the means of putting an end to the horrible social disease of prostitution. The meaning of it is that the man can marry young, the woman can remain self-supporting, and they can have their children later on in life when they are in a position to support them. This is the way, and the only way conceivable, where prosti-

tution can be ended. And yet, to think that our ecclesiastical advisers have caused the passing of laws against the spread of information about it!

It is to be hoped that *The Freewoman* will long continue to do its remarkable work in introducing people, and especially women, to express themselves openly on vital questions.

As a result of the above discussion, several new members that join the League, and many inquiries for advice have been received.

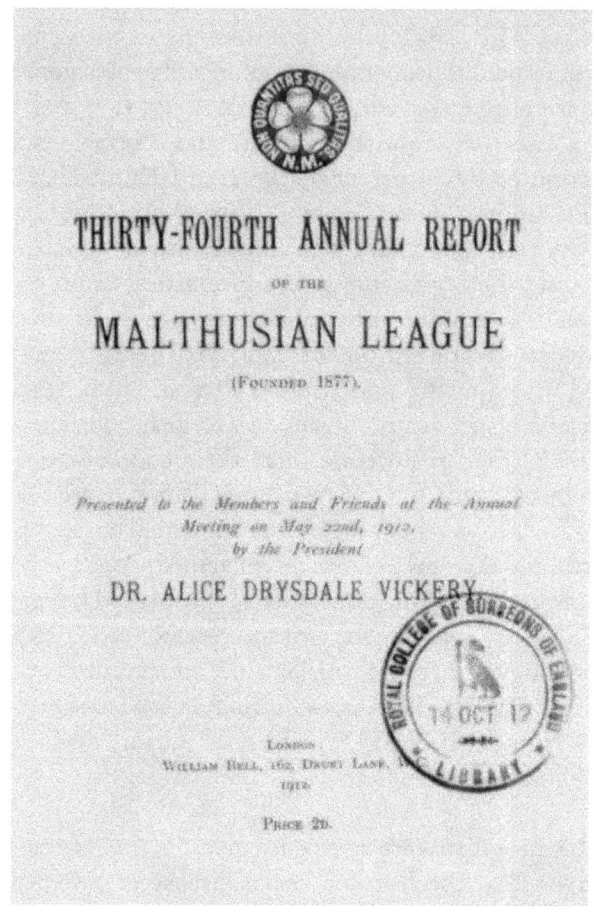

Introduction to "A New Prophetess of Feminism"
Trevor Blake (2019)

The following article is reprinted from *The Forum* Volume XLVIII (July-December 1912) pp 455-464. Frances Maule Bjorkman (1879–1966) was a Heterodite, the self-designation for those in the Heterodoxy group founded by Marie How in 1912 in New York. The Heterodoxy group required its members "not be orthodox in opinion." She was also a resident of the Helicon Colony of Englewood, New Jersey. They raised their children collectively, and in what founder Upton Sinclair called a "spirit of socialism" they shared the upkeep of the Colony (until such time as they did not and hired outside workers). The Helicon Colony was "open to any white person of good moral character" with all that implies. "Not for herself, tho' sweet the air of freedom" is the opening line to the final stanza of the song "Coming" as found in *Suffrage Songs and Verse* by Charlotte Perkins Gilman (New York: Charlton Company 1911). Hertha Ayrton (1854–1923) was a British scientist and suffragist who invented the Ayrton Fan, used to dispel poison gas from British trenches in World War I. Dr. Ayrton's stepdaughter E. Ayrton Zangwill wrote "The Fashioning of Florence Isabel" for *The Freewoman*, perhaps leading to Bjorkman's confusion about "her sister, Mrs. Florence Ayrton Zangwill, wife of Israel Zangwill." The suffragist newspaper *Votes for Women* took on the subtitle "The War Paper for Women" by 1916. The Women's Social and Political Union negotiated with the Primer Minister to suspend all but their publishing work until the end of World War I. The WSPU ended in 1917, a year before the war ended, and eleven years before full women's suffrage in England.

A NEW PROPHETESS OF FEMINISM
FRANCES MAULE BJORKMAN (1912)

A few weeks ago the English newspapers were greatly excited over the report that the suffrage book-shops of London were offering for sale "literature of an abnormal, immoral and dangerous character." The publication mentioned most prominently in this connection, and, obviously, the objective of the whole attack, was a weekly review, less than a year old, called *The Freewoman*. It was charged that this paper stood for "free love," anarchy, and all the other dark and dangerous doctrines to which the mind of the frightened bourgeois public reverts when it sees existing standards challenged. All of which seems to point to *The Freewoman* as a social symptom of unusual interest.

It cannot be dismissed as a mere "crank" publication, for it has already won respectful recognition from such persons as John Galsworthy, H. G. Wells, Charles Granville, Francis Grierson, Mr. and Mrs. Walter M. Gallichan, and Mr. and Mrs. Havelock Ellis—all but the last two of whom have contributed to its pages. Furthermore, it is backed and issued by a publishing house which is distinguished for the high literary quality and the serious purpose of its publications. That it is radical, with a radicalism beyond that of any of the advanced publications of purely masculine manufacture, cannot be denied. It is the last thing we should wish to deny, for it is this very quality of radicalism that makes it so significant and compelling a sign of new developments taking place within the woman movement.

Viewed merely from the standpoint of general journalism, *The Freewoman* is so novel as to arrest attention; and when it is considered in the light of a woman's propagandist organ, it is seen to have a meaning which may quite legitimately be regarded as sinister by the upholders of the existing order.

The charge that it is put forth under the aegis of the suffrage movement, while quite natural, is altogether unjust to the suffragists—that is to say, to the suffragists *as such*. True, its editor, Miss Dora Marsden, first came into prominence as a suffragist. True also that Miss Mary Gawthorpe, whose name, for the first few weeks, stood as co-editor with that of Miss Marsden, is only less celebrated as a suffragist in England than Mrs.-or-Miss Pankhurst. It is also true, however, that the suffragists, and especially the militants, far from welcoming the new journal to their shops, are fighting it with all their might.

The obvious conclusion would be that this was because of the attack on the militant society that was printed in the first number. This did undoubtedly draw forth some violent reprisals. But for the deep and abiding hostility to the new journal on the part of organized suffragism in England, we must look deeper.

The truth of the matter is that *The Freewoman* is "spiking the suffragists' game."

The suffragists, both in England and America, have been trying all these years to convince the public that they were asking to be free only in order that they might serve the more effectively. This is the keynote of the most modern of the suffrage literature and the theme of every suffrage "soap-boxer."

> Not for herself, tho' sweet the air of freedom;
> Not for herself, tho' dear the new-won power;
> But for the child, who needs a nobler mother,
> For the whole people, needing one another—
> Comes woman to her hour.

Nor is this attitude confined to the suffragists. The women who have won nation-wide recognition for their social services—the Jane Addamses and Florence Kelleys—show that their demand for wider opportunities for women is based on their appreciation of women's untapped capacity for "usefulness." Even the prophetesses and philosophers of feminine revolt—more radical because less concerned with the immediate accomplishment of definite ends—have preached "service"—widened and exalted almost beyond recognition, but still service—as the ideal aim of a free womanhood—whether it be the world service of the social mother "with the self-conscious purpose" to "feed and clothe and teach the human race," envisioned by Charlotte Perkins Gilman; whether the exalted and spiritualized personal service of home and man and child insisted upon with such passionate fervor by Ellen Key; or whether the toil with hand and brain in every field of human endeavor which the poetic vision of Olive Schreiner saw as the necessary condition to the preservation of race virility.

So far the Feminists—doers and thinkers both—have played

more or less directly into the hands of the suffragists in their endeavor to allay instinctive masculine fears that if women were to acquire first-hand power, they would use it for the furtherance of their own personal ends instead of applying it—as they have always done, and on the whole so satisfactorily, with their delegated power—to the enhancement of the lives of others.

Then came *The Freewoman* with the incredible heresy that all this was deception—albeit largely unconscious—and that the woman movement was nothing if not an effort on the part of women to lift themselves forever out of the "servant" class and to place themselves definitely and finally among the "masters"—using their faculties, like all masters, for the up building and development of their own personalities and the advancement of their own personal aims.

It admitted freely that this would entail enormous and fundamental changes in the social structure and in the relations of the sexes—that it would involve, first of all, the achievement of absolute economic independence of men by women; the repudiation, by women, of the marriage contract, at least in its present form; developments in domestic labor and administration so vast as to have all the outer aspects of "breaking up the home;" readjustments in the world of politics and industry great enough to accommodate double the present number of productive thinkers and workers, demanding, not only admission, but pay.

Whatever the private views of individual suffragists—and, of course, they vary widely—the raising of these issues at the present juncture when, literally, women's lives are being sacrificed to put through a specific measure, was regarded as nothing less than an act of treachery. The Manchester branch of the Women's Social and Political Union, which Miss Gawthorpe had organized and of which she had been acknowledged leader during the first stormy years of the militant movement, sent resolutions formally condemning the paper. Mrs. Hertha Ayrton, the scientist, as a subscriber to the establishment fund, and her sister, Mrs. Florence Ayrton Zangwill, wife of Israel Zangwill, who had contributed one of her stories to the first number, wrote to demand a formal announcement of the withdrawal of their support. In general, the position of Miss Gawthorpe—who was still ill from injuries sustained in a militant demonstration—was made so painful that, after the first few weeks, she withdrew her name as co-editor although still giving the paper her hearty moral support.

Miss Marsden adopted the opposite policy of staying in the fight and trying to convince the suffragists that no immediate gain was worth having unless founded upon truth and understanding. To this end the paper was thrown open for the discussion of every problem—social and individual; mental, moral, spiritual and physical—affecting women's present position and their aims and prospects for the future.

These discussions are notable for the number and variety of the points of view represented; for the range of the subjects covered; and for the height of the intellectual passion displayed in them; but, of course, what has attracted attention to them has been the candid way in which they have dealt with various problems of sex. Several times, I understand, this has very nearly brought the paper under the ban of the censor. In explanation of *The Freewoman*'s "open" policy on this subject, and in answer to a criticism from a friendly correspondent, Miss Marsden writes:

> This is an odd enough criticism of a journal that calls itself a Feminist review. That it can be made arises from the difficulty of grasping the definition of Feminism, even when specifically defined. Feminism is concerned with the readjustment of the balance of sex relationships, which has been rendered necessary by the age-long acceptance of Masculinism, the present accepted, but not unchallenged theory—a theory which acknowledges the domination of men in sex relationships and in all the various activities and spheres of labor which are accommodated to such. It will thus be seen that we regard Feminism, not as a final doctrine, but as a temporary theory of expedients and readjustments. Masculinism and Feminism are relative terms, and when one is strong enough to equate the other, both will become merged in a common doctrine of Humanism. We assure our correspondent that, both by interest and temperament, we are far more likely to trespass upon the sphere of Humanism than to keep too unduly to the restricted sphere of Feminism.

Despite all opposition the paper has now, in less than a year's time, won for itself a secure position among a small but rapidly growing group of thinking people in England, and is beginning to find support and recognition in America. Out of the interest which it has aroused in the problems of Feminism, a "Freewoman Discussion Circle" has grown, which holds weekly meetings to take up in greater detail the large issues which the paper has merely launched for discussion. It has been able to secure—without pay—contributions from some of the most eminent of living English authors, and it has discovered some young writers of marked gifts.

It is the editorial articles of Miss Marsden herself, however, that not only give the paper its unique quality—its originality, its honesty, its fearlessness—but which chiefly warrant its claim for consideration as a social symptom.

Whatever justification there may be for the charge of the suffragists that *The Freewoman* has jeopardized the immediate granting of votes to women, there is no question that Miss Marsden's editorial articles are serving to lift the woman movement to a higher level of seriousness and importance in the minds of a rapidly growing circle of both men and women readers. She, more than any of the other feministic writers—possibly partly because she is a journalist dealing from week to week with living issues—is making the public realize that the matter is pressing and cannot be made to wait; that it is vital in that it involves half—or more than half—of the whole race; and that it requires for the solution of its problems a degree of enlightenment—especially in the field of modern psychology—which has never yet been applied to it.

This extraordinary young woman has shot into the literary and philosophic firmament as a star of the first magnitude. Although practically unknown except as a settlement worker and a suffragist before the advent of *The Freewoman* last November, she speaks always with the quietly authoritative air of the writer who has arrived. Her style has beauty—at times, great beauty —as well as force and clarity. Merely as an essayist she compels admiration and makes us wonder why we have never heard of her before.

I can give only the most meagre details regarding her personal history. Like so many of the leaders of the English movement, she is a Lancashire woman. To me there is a peculiar significance in the fact that it is the one spot in all England where women's work is economically equivalent with that of men which has produced most of the leaders of feminine revolt. I know that it is in the frontier States in our own country, where women's toil has also been valued equally with the labor of men, that women have been accorded political equality. It would thus seem that the participation of women in the productive work of the world is the factor which creates the atmosphere in which the demand for freedom grows.

Miss Marsden was graduated from Manchester University with the degree of B.A. and took up teaching as her profession, working incidentally in the University Settlement. She seems to have passed through the successive stages of Socialist and Socialist-irritated-with-Socialism common to university settlementers of idealistic temperaments on both sides of the water, and to have arrived finally at a tentative acceptance of Syndicalism.

Immediately after Christabel Pankhurst's first militant protest, Miss Marsden threw herself heart and soul into the militant suffrage movement—even leaving her post as teacher to become an organizer for the Women's Social and Political Union. When challenged to explain this fact in view of her present hostile attitude toward the W. S. P. U., Miss Marsden stated editorially in *The Freewoman* that at that time she believed that she was allying herself with a general woman emancipation movement, which, she found later, was not the case. In the meantime, however, she ran the full gamut of suffragette experiences. She served two months in Holloway Gaol for her all too gallant defence of "the colors" in the clash between the police and the Lancashire women's deputation to the House of Commons in 1909. She went through the hunger strike and was strait-jacketed in Strangeways Gaol in Manchester, where she had been committed for throwing a rock through the glass roof of a hall in which a Cabinet Minister's meeting was in progress, and she was arrested and discharged too many times to count. The newspapers of Lancashire called her "Dauntless Dora."

On the occasion of Winston Churchill's visit to Southport during the campaign of 1909, Miss Marsden succeeded in outwitting the police in the face of the most extraordinary precautions against suffragette interruptions. A large sum had been spent on extra police protection. A solid cordon was drawn up around the hall, and additional guards were stationed at every entrance. The paving stones had been taken up from the streets and set on end for barricades. Yet when Mr. Churchill began to explain that the people ought to support the Government because the Government represented the people, from high up somewhere near the ceiling floated down a thin feminine voice:

It does not represent the women, Mr. Churchill.

Far out through a ventilator above the stage leaned the figure of Dora Marsden, small and slight, and with her thin, intense little face wan and pale from nearly twenty-four hours of fast and vigil. But her voice rose crisp and clear above the uproar, and she coolly proceeded to deliver her message until the stewards, who had at first been utterly demoralized by the interruption, found their way into her loft and dragged her forcibly from the opening. Delighted crowds in the streets saw her thrust through the broken glass of a window and set rolling down the sloping roof—from which she must certainly have fallen had she not found a slight hold in the projecting coping—and then pulled down and hustled off to jail.

During the years from 1908 to 1910, the newspaper of the militant society, *Votes for Women*, was eloquent in praise of her courage, her resourcefulness, her devotion. During 1910 she was mentioned less and less frequently, and at the beginning of 1911 she disappeared from its columns altogether.

It appears that in 1910, she registered a vigorous protest against the exclusive *Votes for Women* policy and urged the inauguration of an aggressive and determined campaign in behalf of the general principles of Feminism—without results, of course. In 1911 she made a similar appeal, and receiving no encouragement, she withdrew from the organization, determined, if necessary, to begin alone the work which she felt was pressing to be done. She was offered the associate editorship of *The Vote*, organ of the rival militant organization, The Women's Freedom League, but after a brief trial, definitely reached the conclusion that the particular end which she had in view could not be accomplished within the movement at all. Accordingly she resigned her office and took up the task of trying to secure from suffragists financial backing for an independent feminist journal. The help was not forthcoming, and, since she had cut herself off from all money-earning activities in order to put through this undertaking, she experienced the most extreme poverty. The project of an independent Feminist journal financed by suffragists was amply demonstrated to be quite out of the question, but just at this point Miss Marsden learned of the willingness of her present publishers to try an experiment in feministic journalism, and *The Freewoman* became a fact.

Miss Marsden's special demand has less to do with the external and material conditions of woman's emancipation than with a fundamental change in woman's point of view toward herself. Miss Marsden's concern is that women shall acquire the habit of appraising their individual worth as "separate spiritual entities," apart from any of their relational aspects. They must learn to judge themselves as individuals and not as mothers, wives, sisters or daughters—not even as "world mothers" or "creators and conservators of life." It is only through acquiring this sense of value, and the courage to sacrifice to the development of their individual gifts everything that threatens such development, that women will make manifest their highest potentialities.

As long as women accept "support" from men, they must be prepared, in return, to sacrifice their own ends and purposes and to forgo the cultivation of their own personalities to advance the interests and to minister to the needs of their "providers." It is only just and fair that they should do this. Therefore, if they are not always to be under obligations and exactions imposed from without, they will of necessity have to earn their own "support" by productive paid labor. They will have to reject the proposal of State endowment for motherhood for the reason that this scheme would merely transfer their obligation toward some individual man to a collective body of men. It follows, then, that they will have to be prepared to support, not only themselves, but any children that they may bring into the world.

> They—the Freewomen—do not wish, by law or by any other means, to fasten their responsibilities on others. They themselves are prepared to shoulder their own. They bear no grudge and claim no exemptions because of the greater burdens which nature has made theirs. They accept them willingly because of their added opportunity and power...
>
> She must produce within herself strength sufficient to provide for herself and for those of whom nature has made her the natural guardian, her children. To this end she must open up resources of wealth for herself. She must work, earn money. She must seize upon the incentives which have spurred men on to strenuous effort—wealth, power, titles and public honor...
>
> It is neither desirable nor necessary for women, when

they are mothers, to leave their chosen, money-earning work for any length of time. The fact that they so often do so rests largely upon a tradition that will have to be worn down. In wearing it down vast changes must take place in social conditions, in housing, nursing, kindergarten, education, cooking, cleaning, in the industrial world and in the professions. These changes will have for their motive the accommodation of such conditions as will enable women to choose and follow a life-work, apart from, and in addition to, their natural function of reproduction.

Miss Marsden makes it quite clear that she fully understands how hard is her doctrine and how limited must be its appeal. For generations, perhaps, only the "exceptional" women—the geniuses and the artists, women who are driven by an inner necessity to recognize and to cultivate their gifts—will follow it. But that the strenuous effort that it implies will be good for women, *and for their children*, she has no manner of doubt.

> We believe that it is to the Freewomen that we have to look for the conscious setting toward a higher race, for which their achievements will help to make ready, and their strivings and aspirations help to mould. For this, they do not require protection; they need liberty. They do not require ease; they need strenuous effort.
> They will have to strive, and that they should so strive will be well for them and for their children.

So, in the end, it appears that it is by casting aside the old passive role of self-sacrifice and following the path of self-realization that women are to become "useful" in the highest sense of all, to serve in the most exalted possible capacity.

J. WILLIAM LLOYD

John William Lloyd (1857—1940) was an individualist anarchist poet and author. Lloyd founded *The Free Comrade*, a magazine edited by Clarence Lee Swartz published between 1900 and 1902. *The Free Comrade* championed anarchism, free love, Whitman ("Our American Shakespeare, and greater than he") and Edward Carpenter ("The greatest man of modern England"). Lloyd wrote two utopian novels, *The Natural Man / A Romance of the Golden Age* (Newark: Benedict Prieth 1902) and *The Dwellers in Vale Sunrise / How They Got Together and Lived Happy Ever After, a Sequel to 'The Natural Man,' Being an Account of the Tribes of Him* (Westwood: Ariel Press 1904).

The Free Comrade resumed publication in a new series from 1910 to 1912. Lloyd now co-edited it with his friend Leonard D. Abbott, who financed its publication. Between the end of the original series and the beginning of the new, Lloyd had stopped considering himself ananarchist, instead joining the Socialist Party. He wrote: "I am still anarchistic in the essential sense… the great need of Socialism is a stronger infusion of Anarchism… " Meanwhile his friend Abbott had moved from socialism towards anarchism. They offered the new series "as an advocate of the juncture of the Anarchist and Socialist forces."

Lloyd wrote hundreds of poems, many of which appeared in anarchist periodicals. He was published in Benjamin Tucker's *Liberty*; in Moses Harman's anarchist and free love journal *Lucifer the Light Bearer*; the anarchist and sex-radical newspaper *Fair Play* and others.

Photograph of J. Wm. Lloyd with book in front of fireplace featuring devilish andirons, 1927. Care of Lorne Bair Rare Books.

Introducing a Review of *What is Mutualism?* 39
Wendy McElroy   *(2008)*
Trevor Blake   *(2019)*

Anarchist-Mutualism. 40
J. William Lloyd   *(1927)*

Photograph of J. William Lloyd in California 52
J. William Lloyd   *(N.D.)*

A Brief Sketch of the Life of J. William Lloyd. 53
J. William Lloyd   *(1940)*
Continuing the publication of original source material on *Liberty* contributor John William Lloyd, I attached herewith an autobiographical essay entitled "A Brief Sketch of the Life of J. William Lloyd" — of course, by Lloyd himself.
                                   –Wendy McElroy, http://www.wendymcelroy.com

Lecture to the Ferrer Colony 57
J. William Lloyd   *(N.D.)*
Another transcription of original source material from *Liberty* contributor John William Lloyd. This is the text of a speech that Lloyd delivered to the members of the Ferrer Colony.
                                   –Wendy McElroy, http://www.wendymcelroy.com

Introducing a Review of *What is Mutualism?*
Wendy McElroy (2008)
Trevor Blake (2019)

I recently transcribed several essays of J. Wm Lloyd, a frequent contributor to Benjamin Tucker's individualist anarchist periodical *Liberty* (1881) through most of its lifespan. Lloyd was the author of several works, mostly of poetry, that were heavily promoted by Liberty; they included "The Anarchists' March," *The Dwellers in Vale Sunrise*, and *The Red Heart in a White World*. To the extent there is a poet laureate of individualist anarchism, it is surely John William Lloyd. I consider this to be a companion piece to Lloyd's classical essay on Anarchist Socialism. [W. McE.]

∉

Clarence Lee Swartz (1868–1936) was the publisher of egoist journal *I* (1898) and the author of *What is Mutualism?* (New York: Vanguard Press 1927). Pierre-Joseph Proudhon (1809 –1865) was a communist anarchist. Benjamin R. Tucker (1854–1939) was the publisher of *Liberty* (1881) and published the first English-language translation of Max Stirner's *Der Einzige und sein Eigentum* as *The Ego and His Own* in 1907. "The Anarchists' March" was a song set to the tune of the Finnish war song *björneborgarnes marsch*. It was published as sheet music by Benjamin R. Tucker in 1888. While the concept of humanism has deeper roots, the first humanist society was founded by Charles Potter in 1927, the same year that Lloyd describes himself as a Humanist. Also published in 1927 was the Dill Pickle Press edition of *Might is Right* by Ragnar Redbeard, a concept that Lloyd objects to in this essay. [T.B.]

Anarchist-Mutualism
J. William Lloyd (1927)

My old-time comrade and dear friend, C. L. Swartz, has sent me a copy of his new book, "What is Mutualism", for review. I have unlimited respect for C. L. Swartz, his ripe scholarship and sincere idealism, and if I am compelled by an equal sincerity to differ with him, I hope our valued friendship will not be affected.

I make this review with pleasure, because it will incidentally afford me an opportunity to explain myself to my old comrades, who, I know, regard me as a sad renegade. In 1884, or thereabout, I became a disciple of the school of Proudhon and Tucker. Tho never very orthodox, I passed for a pretty straight Individualist-Anarchist for some 20 years. Tucker was a gentleman and a scholar, and his personal charm held me as well as intellectual and moral conviction. But at last my critical faculties were turned on the cult itself and I had to come out. I am no longer an Anarchist, but perhaps on many points I might fairly be called a Near-Anarchist still. I no longer label myself an Anarchist, or a Socialist (except in the large use of that term), but a Humanist, and the one principle I subscribe to is the greatest benefit to the greatest number. But I want all the personal liberty it is possible to have, for myself and others, so far as it is consistent with social benefit. I say all this because this new cult of Mutualism is simply the old cult of Tuckerism, of Individualist-Anarchism, under a new name and very wisely supplemented by the constructive principle of cooperation. As such it is far more attractive to me, as Co-operation is the most saving word in the language.

The Anarchists of half a century ago knew nothing of the psychology of modern business. With a new idea to put over, and in private life, courteous, cordial and refined, on paper they were a lot of swaggering, critical, swashbucklers, arrogant, browbeating and insulting, and all who differed were knaves or fools, and frankly so informed. The dictionary was reversed, and the astonished world was told that Anarchy was Order and Government was Invasion. Worse salesmanship for a new propaganda could hardly have been conceived. But conceit did not stop here, for men were also told that the Declaration of Independence must also be reversed. There were no "natural rights", or any rights except those of might, unless created by contract between associates, and that children were the chattels of their parents, who (after all, as it was contradictorily discovered) had a natural right to do what they pleased with them as a labor product. It was a thousand pities, for those men really had some very valuable ideas that the world needed and which a sane and considerate propaganda might have enabled them to spread far. The tone of "What is Mutualism" is very different. It is courteous, persuasive, respectful and sweetly reasonable, and the old, antagonism-creating name has been wisely dropped, but under this gentle exterior one is saddened to see most of the old ideas reappear still.

As I see it: —

>Liberty is to do as you please;
>Law is that which limits liberty;
>Government is that which applies law.

There is not now, and never has been, any complete liberty in our natural world or among men.

The universe is constructed of opposites, which always operate co-existently, at least to some extent; therefore liberty and authority always co-exist and operate together,

Anarchists plead only for equal-liberty, which is limited liberty, and therefore admit at the start that there is something in Nature and her necessities which limits liberty; therefore admit natural law and natural government—that there is a natural basis and origin for government. It is a dangerous admission for their cult. But they go further and claim that even equal-liberty has no rights against invasive might and its right must be created by an artificial contract between associates who pool their mights to defend it. They don't stress the corollary, but if cornered admit it, that those outside the contract have no rights whatever and may be invaded without guilt by whosoever has the might. It is remindful of the morality of our Amerindians who are angels in tribal relations and fiends on the warpath to outsiders. They thus create a justification for invasion that the moral sense of the rest of men denies—and so still further cease to be the champions of liberty.

It is a tremendous strategic mistake that the Mutualists thus make to fly in the face of and array against them the moral intuitions of mankind. And quite unnecessary also. Even if they believe this, it is needless to mention it. Nobody suspects for a moment that Comrade Swartz and his immediate associates are seeking excuses for rape and murder on non-associates, or that they would treat their children any more like puppies or stove wood than other humans. Why then metaphysically outrage the moral code of those they are trying to persuade? What they are trying to put over is that good men, if they wish to have satisfactory liberty, must associate to realize and defend it. Why not emphasize that and chuck offensive hair-splitting out of the window? Why take a position that would theoretically permit one of their associates to prey as a burglar on non-associates, or a woman to sell her pretty little daughter into white slavery? And if it actually happened, if the man and the woman were loyal and inoffensive within the clan, and willing that the other members had equal liberty to burglarize and sell, how, without violating their principles, could they act to stop it? It was precisely at this point where Tucker, mad with his logic, asserted that the child was the labor-product of the mother, therefore absolutely her property and that the mother had the right to throw her baby into the fire, like an old newspaper, if she chose, that I broke with him first, and my Anarchism first began to crack. What insanity has moved modern Mutualists to re-assert these positions against which the heart of humanity and the intuitions of its moral conscience will always rebel? Especially as it is quite certain that none of those writing this book (for I am informed it is a mutualist creation) intend to make any practical application of such anti-social dogmas; nor has the practical application of the theory of the social-contract any need of such logic.

Nothing seems easier to demonstrate than natural rights. When Nature created us she endowed us all with an innate and indestructible conviction that we have:—

1. A right to live;
2. A right to promote and defend that life;
3. A right to do anything that really benefits us.

These are our natural rights, and everybody is convinced of them, spite of all doctrinaires. It is safe to say that Comrade Swartz is as convinced of his natural right to these rights as I am and would fight as hard to maintain them. And there are other natural rights with a wider social application. If advanced thinkers base their contentions on natural rights, and claim these for all human beings by the very fact of their humanity, they can go ahead with confidence and appeal with results to the human heart.

Those who would reason clearly on the question of rights should always make a distinction between rights and privileges. The so-called "right of might" is in the nature of a privilege. It is not a right, nor is it right unless it serves a right. Our rights always relate to benefits and connote satisfaction. That is right which benefits. In Nature might has no justification for action unless it secures benefit—therefore is subordinate to right. Might must serve right before it is justified and right must have the service of might before it can practically act, tho it existed just as certainly before. Swartz has a right to his Mutual Bank, tho he has no might to compel the government to withdraw its impediments. If might does not serve right, Nature condemns it in the final results—they are not beneficial. By endorsing the right of might Anarchists throw away their whole case, for they thereby endorse and justify all successful invasions, and particularly the invasions of government, which has the most might.

Instead of all rights being derived from might, all rights are derived from benefit and imply that, otherwise cannot qualify.

Government has its origin in Nature below man. Animal parents control their young, animal packs follow and obey a leader. We see the same among primitive men. Nature has instituted an instinct for government and its purpose has been benefit and preservation. The mother governs her child for the benefit of the family; and the tribe, the larger family, huddles for protection under the strength, courage and wisdom of the chief. The natural roots of government are in the mother and the chief, and in that self-government by which a man conserves his health and safety by controlling his dangerous appetites and impulses. Government of this kind is instinctively sought by human beings, and benefits of this sort are instinctively expected of government; and where benefits of this sort are derived from government, there need be no fear of rebellion. To "establish justice, insure domestic tranquility, provide for the common defence, promote the general welfare, and secure the blessings of liberty", states the essentials pretty well.

Government of the invasive kind began when tribesmen adopted these very principles that Tucker and Swartz would have us accept—they felt an implied contract bound them together in loyalty within the tribe, but outside there was no right but might, no one outside the tract had any rights they were required to respect. The result was invasions, war, conquest of weaker tribes, property in loot, the ownership of stolen lands, the making of slaves. The chief made himself king over these conquered ones, subjects. By a separate contract with his strongest warriors he divided stolen lands among them, and made them feudal lords with serfs, and bound them to him and away from the loyalty to the weaker ones of the tribe. Special privileges in stolen property—that has been the quality of invasive government ever since. But the people have never forgotten that government purely for social benefit is perfectly possible, and the reason they do not forget it is because they still have mothers, and still at times, strong friends and champions arise to use their might to protect them.

Another instance where an implied contract was used for invasion was when men usurped all rights in the name of might, declared women had no rights, subjugated them, and instituted that form of marriage in which, in its pure form, the woman was forced to be monogamous, was purely her husband's property, without human rights, and her children also property and also his.

Pure liberty—the untrammeled doing as one pleases—nowhere exists. Law and government, in some form or degree, open or concealed, always accompany liberty and modify it. When Anarchists ask only for equal-liberty they themselves acknowledge this and institute a degree of law and government by limiting liberty by equality, governing liberty by equality. Once you admit that, in practice, liberty must be limited, law and government are admitted, and it only becomes a question how much or how little liberty is best for the greatest benefit. If Mutualists bind themselves by a contract, the moment any one of them finds he has made a mistake and no longer agrees to the contract, he finds that the Contract has become a Government, and its several parts are laws, which its associates will enforce upon him. He can leave of course but if his home and investments are there that will not be so easy, and if obliged to go to another group, under another contract, he only changes governments, as an American who goes to Canada or Mexico. If a child has the misfortune to be born under one of these contract-mutualisms he finds he has no rights whatever, and is only property of his parent's might. Not even equal-liberty for him until big enough to put his head into one of those contract nooses. If he chooses to live as a pure inoffensive individualist, outside of any contract, he will find that for his mutualist neighbors he has no rights whatever, unless they choose to endow him with some. If not, they are free to exercise their might upon him.

If a contract exactly expresses the will of a member it, of course, does not govern him. But it is a rigid form, for all that, and, sooner or later is bound to pinch somewhere, for he is growing and changing. When it pinches it governs, and if he enforces it on his dissenting desires he aids it to govern, but it governs none the less. If he does not enforce it on himself, but breaks it, and others enforce it on him, he is sure it governs. If enforced only by forfeiture of bonds, loss of privileges, etc., it governs still. A contract enforced limits liberty, tho not necessarily equal-liberty, and a contract not enforced, or not intended for enforcement, is weak, and weak precisely at points of greatest strain. And it is safe to say that, with any contract involving social life, there will be moments of emergency and crucial necessity when imperious wills will enforce the contract or violate it spite of any scruples about equal-liberty.

Perhaps the contract will be enforced only by the boycott. Mutualists would fain [sic] persuade us that there is no possible invasion of equal liberty in a boycott. Comrade Swartz, instinctively sensing a weak spot in his levees here, throws all his strength to its support. "It is", he says, "the only weapon that cannot be used invasively. The reason for this is that the boycott is not an act; it is merely the refusal to act." Yet please note that he admits it is a "weapon", and implies that it can be "used", and on page 163 admits that a boycotted person "may correctly allege that he has been coerced", and lower down speaks of a boycott exerting a "pressure." On page 165, we see it recommended as a "punishment for crime", and a "drastic penalty", "more painful to many than to be incarcerated in a prison", etc. Now how can the use of a weapon, to exert a pressure, to coerce, to inflict a drastic penalty or punishment, worse than incarceration in a prison, be described as no act, "merely a declination to act"? It is absurd. The confusion of the Anarchist here comes from his failing to understand that, in the paradoxicality of the universe, there are acts-negative as well as acts-positive, and that the boycott is one of the acts-negative. A failure, or refusal to act in a positive manner may still be an act-negative. Thus if a baby, at my feet, falls into a ditch, and I, quite able to retrieve it, allow it to drown, I am just as guilty of its murder as if I pushed it under; if I see a spark starting to ignite a house, and I, quite able, indifferently permit it to burn on, I am morally guilty of arson. When I boycott or ostracize a person to coerce him to do something which he is unwilling to do I am acting, and my act is an act of government.

For this is precisely what government is—in the relations of human beings, it is the action of one mind to control another mind to coerce it to perform an act, or cease to act, where it is reluctant or unwilling to comply—that is government, and is so understood by all mankind—or, more briefly—government is the imposition of a stronger will upon a weaker will that is here unwilling. It is always a limitation of liberty, even if intended to maintain whatever liberty may be possible.

Anarchists will find, whenever they try to apply their theories, that they cannot maintain an orderly, comfortable home, or run an orderly, harmonious school, or conduct an orderly public meeting, (Tucker averred that it was necessary that the moderator should be an autocrat), or run a safe railroad train, or sail a safe ship, without government. There must be discipline for order and efficiency—self-applied, or externally applied, and almost invariably the latter, for the self-applied is very unreliable in practice. Swartz praises the superior efficiency of private business concerns over government action in the same lines. He fails to note that the reason is that the discipline and government of the business enterprises is far more instant and severe than that of ordinary political government. In the army and navy, where government is still more strict and severe, efficiency is supreme. Efficiency is apt to be in inverse proportion to liberty. But of course government is a blind force and must be directed by intelligence; a fool must not be an engineer.

I cite all this merely to prove that Anarchism is a natural impossibility. Government is ubiquitous and pops up everywhere. There is no such thing as complete liberty, and equal-liberty, tho a beautiful moral standard, as an ideal, is, in real life invaded all the time, by stern natural necessity. There is no such thing as an "individual sovereign", a "single, separate person"—he does not exist. Centrally there is a certain nucleus of individuality, yes, and very precious to us, but on all borders and contacts one merges with forces, things and persons, depends on them, and becomes all tangled up, coercing and being coerced, governing and being governed, in all sorts of conscious or unconscious, secret or overt ways, by acts-negative or acts-positive. Society is not a mere word, but a living reality. As soon as any group forms there begins to develop a collective, composite spirit, or mind, invisible, but very real, that more or less telepathically unites and includes it—all its members. All contribute life to it—all are influenced, modified by it. This is Society—the composite spirit of the group—and it exercises an invisible, but very real government. The visible leaders must mainly express it or they do not last long. There is always a majority rule, tho a powerful individual mind may captivate the majority, at least for a time. Anarchists cannot escape the action of this government; moreover they will participate in it.

I first really faced the fallacy of Anarchism when I faced the problem of Conservation. When Anarchists forgot the assertion of the single right of might, they were full of rights to assert, and one was that the individual sovereign had an indisputable right to go to wild Nature for anything he could use and, provided he left the field open for others, no one had a right to prevent him. I agreed, till suddenly I realized that this meant that an Italian could live on slaughtered son gbirds, a market pot-hunter could kill all the year round, fish could be seined out of all waters, the lumber-hog could seep away the forests, and, as long as these men left equal-liberty for others to commit equal havoc, there was absolutely nothing in Anarchist principles that could consistently be applied to stop them. They were occupying and using, and not invading equal-liberty—and to stop them was "government", that is, "invasion". I dropt Anarchism right then and there. I began to see emerging the rights of society—of a wise collectivity, envisaging the rights of all and of posterity. Some social benefits required even the sacrifice of equal-liberty.

In presenting their propaganda, Anarchists seem to fight shy of putting out any definite program, or telling in unmistakable terms how their principles would work out in practice. Usually they prefer to only deliver fascinating generalities. One of these fascinating generalities is that of usufruct, which, they claim, would give a perfect title to land. But when you look into it, this doctrine of occupation and use is as full of potential trouble as any tropical jungle. Will occupancy alone give a full title to ownership, or will use alone do so, or must it be both occupancy and use? And what constitutes either occupancy or use? If I set my house in the middle of a quarter-section do I occupy all that land, or do I occupy only what my house actually covers? If I run a footpath over a farm and walk over it frequently, does that constitute use? If I fence in 10,000 acres of rich land, capable of feeding 40,000 people under intensive cultivation, and merely pasture 10,000 head of cattle on the tract, is that occupancy and use and must the other 39,999 leave me in possession? What constitutes failure to occupy? How long may I be absent, and under what circumstances, and still retain occupancy. And so on and so on, and so on? What has the right to decide such questions anyway, or to enforce decisions when made, especially when "the natural right of might" looms in the background? Is it not instantly clear that any and all decisions must be more or less arbitrary? And all occupancy and use of land is to a certain extent a monopoly and excludes some one from the equal right to occupy and use it—is, to a degree, a violation of equal freedom. I see endless possibilities of disputes, quarrels, litigation, fights, feuds, arising out of this utterly loose and indeterminate way of deciding land titles. Far better in every way, in my judgment, is the plan of the Single Taxer—all the people own the land in common and the government administers it; you pay your rent to a clearly defined piece of land, and so long as you pay, you occupy—when you stop payment, you have vacated your title. It is all as clear as dollars and cents, and settled instantly on business-like principles. And makes it far more difficult to hold valuable and socially-needed lands for selfish pleasure or inferior use. Under usufruct a stubborn occupant, holding a strategic position, refusing to sell out, could block a road, even a railroad, and cause expense and trouble, or exact his own price, or exact a toll. Nothing of that [is] possible under government ownership.

Much more could be said, but I have not been asked to write a volume. And there is much in the book to praise. The criticism of Bolshevism is penetrative and deserved. I am not a financier but The Mutual Bank appeals to me as an excellent institution. For many years I have been convinced that the finances of the country should represent and be based upon the exchangeable wealth of the country, not based on gold. The explanation of what The Mutual Bank is, and would do, seems to me to be more clearly given in this book than in anything else I have read. Some such method is painfully needed to deliver from the robbery of interest and insure general prosperity. [NOTE inserted in hand by Lloyd: Now (1934) I believe, with Bellamy, that the remedy is to abolish all banks and money.] The tone of the book is excellent, its literary merit of the highest. There is a complete absence of violent accusation and insult toward opponents, or those criticised. Its working methods, as recommended—education, passive resistance, to repeal obnoxious laws where possible and ignore where impossible—all these are admirable. But repeal would require voting—do Mutualists use the vote? Are they wise enough to be opportunists and to use the enemy's weapons where available? The original Anarchists would die first.

For myself I am satisfied that education and evolution are all we can look to for effective help—the evolution of character. When the general character of society reaches a high enough development, only men of character can represent it in government or serve it in business, and the nature of all institutions will reflect that character, opportunities for the unscrupulous to use the might of force or cunning to domineer and exploit there will always be, under any system, rule or contract, and nothing but the refusal of the tempted to utilize these opportunities can save the day. And no matter how bad the social system, the good man will at once proceed to reform it into one of real social service. Even a dictator is harmless if his character is high enough, and the loudest professor of Anarchism will be a tyrant and a parasite if his character is low enough.

I quite agree with this book in its denunciation of monopoly and special business privilege. Government should never be permitted to create these. I am for free trade and free competition. Private parties should always be free to compete with the government in rendering public service—a competition between government and private companies should act as a corrective of the usual faults of each. I favor the abolition of patents and copyrights, still I think it would be to the public interest to offer inducements to investors. I would suggest a plan something like this: Suppose a board of experts nominated by the manufacturers of the county, to pass on the merits of inventions. Any inventor who chooses may submit his invention to these. If they approve, they appraise the labor cost of his invention, and of his model, and reimburse him for this. They also describe and illustrate his invention in one issue of a periodical they print, which goes to all manufacturers. Any and all are now free to make and sell the invention, but all who do so must pay the inventor a small royalty for his lifetime, or for the time they continue so to do. By this plan the inventor would get at least something for his invention, at least get back his expenses. But it would be the property of the people, and could not be bought up and shelved. All would have access to it on equal terms, and the more who were benefited, the more the inventor would get. And the more good, free inventions, the more the whole world gains.

I fully agree that juries should try yhe law as well as the evidence. In other words, all laws relating to crime should be flexible, and applied or modified according to the peculiar circumstances of each case. Only thus can justice be done. But to select ignorant and unwilling men, haphazard, for jurors, is a most clumsy and dangerous method. Jurymen should be professionals, men of selected character, especially educated in human psychology and the problems of impartial equity; in the employ of the whole people at a fixed salary, and always on the job, trying all cases as they came. Lawyers, too, should be only in the employ of the people, at fixed salaries; not mercenaries, fighting like soldiers of fortune for the highest bidder. The chief business of lawyers should be to settle quarrels, reconcile disputants, dissipate litigation and reform criminals. Also to constantly simplify, clarify and lessen law and save legal expense to the community. For a lawyer to aid a known criminal to escape conviction should be regarded as a worse crime than that of his client, because treasonable to his profession and not against an individual but the whole people.

I am convinced that private associations for defence against crime would swiftly lead to worse abuses than those we now suffer from in that line. Like mercenary lawyers, the temptation would always be to fight for their customers, right or wrong. And to get into conflicts between themselves that might easily embroil the whole community or lead to civil wars. Besides, there is nothing in true Anarchist principles that requires anyone to employ a defence-association. An individual sovereign has a right, according to his principles, to make his own laws about his own affairs, and avenge his own wrongs in his own way. Under Anarchism we could not fail to go back to the old ways of blood-vengeance and the vendetta, to lynch law and standing feuds.

The government we are under today has grown out of the composite spirit of the people and represents it. It is as good as the people deserve, speaking generally, however hard on advanced individuals. It will improve as the spirit of the people improves, and it can only improve that way. Bloody revolutions only deceptively change surfaces. Witness that in modern Russia the continuing spirit of czarist days comes out in despotisms, bureaucracy, massacres, executions without trial, espionage, censorship, corruption, inefficiency. Only those improvements have been made that the spirit of the people was ready for and would peacably have gradually effected anyway.

The greatest reform needed in government is flexibility and a recognition and promotion of growth. If governments were wise they would emasculate and "denature" rebellions by allowing safety-valves and vent-holes for radicals. They would encourage and solicit criticism and assist those who offered better ways to demonstrate their methods in practice, thus submitting them to the acid test. If a new theory could demonstrate actual improvement, then the referendum. No revolutions on that road, but steady evolution.

The trouble with Radicals is that they are practically all doctrinaires. They denounce compromise, not recognizing that compromise is the road of progress. In real life all principles must, at times, recognize and employ their opposites. There is everything in the universe and a time, place and use for each thing. Take the principle of Equal-Freedom and the case of the motorist. The motorist is not a criminal, nor intends to be—simply a busy man, rushing to his important destination, asking only liberty to do so at his own risk, and willing to give the same liberty to everyone, in cars or on foot. But at the crossing of the ways, there stands the traffic-officer, with his white gloves, imperiously stopping and starting him at his will. It is a clear invasion of equal-liberty and he would defy it if he dared, but there is Law behind the officer, and bullets behind the law. Yet there is public benefit in the traffic-officer and the people will never let him go, principle or no principle.

I have been sorry to criticize this book. Its spirit is fine—the spirit of individualist-anarchism usually is fine and co-operation is all to the good. I am for co-operation to the limit and for individual liberty as far as practicable. I agree with Jefferson that the least government that will do the work is the best and would reduce law to a minimum—but social action without some government and some law is naturally impossible and will always be found so. And liberty is the legal-tender of life and a piece of it is the price we pay for every motion and benefit.

Photograph of J. William Lloyd in California
J. William Lloyd (N.D.)

Care of Labadie Photograph Collection, University of Michigan.

A Brief Sketch of the Life of J. William Lloyd
J. William Lloyd (1940)

I was born on June 4th, 1857, at the tiny village of Westfield, New Jersey, (about 20 miles from New York City), of British, immigrant parents, who were almost unschooled, but not illiterate; my father a carpenter, my mother a seamstress.

A last and belated child in the family (the next eleven years older), I was brought up in a clearing in the woods, alone mostly, in the day time, with my mother, with only a few and occasional playmates. Went, in the winters, beginning at the age of seven, to two little, country, one-room, one-teacher schools, to be taught by "rote" the "four R's", tho I was always the school's dunce in "'rithmetic." Left school at 14 to earn my living by hard work. Never so much as heard of High School, unknown at that time in those parts. My education has come from life and the reading of books and an innate flair for literary style.

Did farm work first, then was apprenticed to the carpenter's trade but after one year carpentry collapsed in the "panic" of 1873. Took up gardening, but the second year a late drought destroyed my garden. Then worked my way thru the Hygieo-Therapeutic College of drugless medication, at Florence, New Jersey, which system I later practiced in Kansas, Iowa, Tennessee and Florida. Lacking means, became next a pioneer on the Kansas frontier; first as a worker on a cattle-ranch, cow-punching and prairie-breaking; later on my own homestead. With help of a friend, built myself a little stone cabin, and the girl I had become engaged to at the college, (Maria Elizabeth Emerson, a distant relative of Ralph Waldo) came out from Boston and married me in 1879. We were most happy together, but continuous drought from several years gave us very hard times. No work anywhere. Lived on whole-wheat bread, from borrowed wheat, and milk, with occasional prairie-chicken or rabbit. Only cash we had was $2.00 a month sent from my home. Local doctor, but almost no patients in that hardy and destitute population. Finally accepted invitation from head of Sanitarium at Vinton, Iowa, (who had heard of me from my articles in Medical Journals), to be assistant physician there and left Kansas, successful experience, but institution finally failed from accumulated debts. Followed another invitation to a Health Colony in the mountains of Tennessee. Again hard times. Built myself a beautiful little log cabin and cleared some land, worked in a saw-mill, had a few patients, drove a milk wagon, peddled home-made yeast. All would not suffice, work gave out, colony failed, and I sold out and moved to a similar colony in Florida, "Waldena." Cleared a five-acre lot there, and built myself a two-story log-house, 40×16 splitting out all the shakes for the roof, and all the pickets for my garden, with a "frow." Practiced medicine, but again folks were too healthy and too poor for any profit. Hoed in orange groves for neighbor and one winter cleared 15 acres of pine forest for him. But their colony failed too, work gave out, and I moved to Palatka and worked on a poultry farm. While there Yellow-fever struck Florida as a plague, the State was quarantined, and my beautiful married life ended by my wife dying from some mysterious internal disease, probably cancer of the liver. So, as soon as I could leave the State, I had to take my two little children (a boy born in Kansas and a girl in Tenn.), back to my parental home in N.J., to be cared for by my sister.

To find employment was imperative, and as my school of medicine was recognized there I became a nurse in New York City, specializing on the care of the insane, and also giving massage. My parents soon died, and with the help of my sister and my children, I tried to establish a little chicken-farm, on the old place, on the side.

When in Kansas I had written for the local newspaper and some Medical Journals, in Florida I had written for radical journals and reform papers, and always, ever since I was in college, I wrote poems, almost as a habit (still a habit in my eighties), but now, in New York, I began to bring out books and take literature more seriously, my first book, *Wind-Harp Songs* appearing in 1896, and others gradually following: the most important, *Dawn-Thought* in 1908 and its sequel, *Life's Beautiful Battle*, in 1910.

On March 7th, 1907, my Oriole, my lovely, beautiful daughter and dearest comrade, herself a fine poet and starting a printing-shop of her own, who had always seemed so healthy, died suddenly in Pennsylvania, from appendicitis and peritonitis. One of the great blows of my life. And my sister, Emily, so devoted to me, died in 1912. I had contracted a second marriage in 1901, but that had been unfortunate; we were incompatible, and after first separating were finally divorced. I would have been alone, but my son, who had become a dentist, and married, brought his wife to our home, and we all lived there till 1922. At my sister's death I had inherited the old home.

In 1913, on sudden impulse, and accompanied at first by my bosom friend, Leonard D. Abbott, I started to make a knapsack trip over the British Islands. We went over much of Ireland together, had a period in England, and had just entered Scotland, when the sudden death of his father, forced Leonard to return, I went over most of England, making my headquarters with Dr. John Johnston and the Whitmanites of Bolton. Johnston had written a book on Whitman and was the physician of Edward Carpenter. I spent two days with Carpenter, incidentally meeting Henry S. Salt, the biographer of Thoreau. Also two weeks with William Atkinson, the dear old naturalist of Midhurst, in Sussex, studying the birds of England. A dear, affectionate old man, and what good times we had, tramping the commons and downs. Went into Surrey. Went to Gilbert White's "Selborne." Went to Stonehenge and to Stratford-on-Avon. Visited William Platt, an English poet, went to Chichester and to Chester. Over Devonshire to Glovelly, over all the lake Country. To Winchester and Salisbury. To Milton's Cottage and to Wordsworth's Cottage, and to the old meeting house of William Penn. Hiked over North Wales, and over Snowdown with knapsack on back. Over Isle of Man, and Isle of Wight, and Guernesye and Jersey in the Channel. Spent a day at St. Malo in Brittney. Slipped over to Switzerland and saw the Matterhorn. Visited Havelock Ellis in London and started a friendship lasting till death. Again in Scotland saw all the Burns country in Ayrshire, going out to Afton Water on one trip, seeing Burn's Cottage and birthplace. And, standing on the Brig-'O-Doon, felt the full thrill of the place and how he must have loved it. Went up the Caledonian Canal to Inverness, incidentally climbing Ben Movis, the highest mountain in the British Isles, and making snowballs there in August. Sailed, for a rip, out of Oban to see Fingal's Cave, and Iona's holy Isle, catching a glimpse, from the sea, of the Isle of Skye, with its dark and tragic peaks.

Returning to Glasgow from this trip, I took ship on the Allen Line for Canada, going up the St. Lawrence, stopping a short time at Quebec and spending several days at Montreal, with Horace Traubel at the hospitable home the Bains. Then came home by way of Boston, going out to Wellesly to see my friends, the Dentons.

Altogether I was gone about four months, at a total cost of about

$400.00 and having one of the most delightful experiences of my whole life. And getting just ahead of the World War.

Back in 1903, (something I forgot to tell in its right place) I had gone out to the Pima Indians of Arizona, on the invitation of one tribe to get their wonderful old legends, living with them, as one of them, and building these stories into my *Am-Am-Tam Indian Nights* and some of the experience into *The Songs of the Desert*; on my return visiting the Grand Canyon of the Colorado and the Petrified Forest at Adama; La Veta and Denver, Colorado, Pike's Peak and the Garden of the Gods.

But I had not seen enough of my beloved West and in 1915, I bought a special trip ticket to the California Fairs, on the way seeing Salt Lake City, Yellowstone Park, the Columbia River, Shasta, and going out, after the Fair, from San Francisco to Yosemite and the Mariposa Grove; then two weeks with Dutch friends near Santa Cruz, and some days with other friends at Santa Barbara, thence down to Los Angeles, friends there, and all the sights and cities of Southern California, including the San Diego Fair. On the home-stretch visiting a dear friend at Prescott, Arizona.

In 1922, my son who was going to California to live persuaded me to sell out and do the same. And this brought me finally to Freedom Hill. In 1925 I visited the Society Islands. And the rest of the story is in my *Like an Old Chinese Poet*, accurately told there.

My books are not popular and no publisher wants to risk them but they get extravagant praise from the greater minds, and brought me all my great friends. And in various ways, at my own expense, or from the subsidies of devoted friends, some twenty have gotten into print, and I have unpublished manuscripts to make as many more, which may be published after my death—who knows? Dead is often a man's best advertisement. And it can't be long now, for I am nearing 83, and the lightning keeps hitting closer.

Lecture to the Ferrer Colony
John William Lloyd (N.D.)

In reading this paper to you, members of the Ferrer Colony, I wish to say that I claim neither inspiration nor infallibility. I do not pretend to be an expert in anything. I am simply a friend and a comrade who has a few suggestions to make out of his own thought and experience. It is your part to criticize and reject the useless.

In coming to a colony, you are aiming at a more ideal social life. Were it not so there would be no object in your forming a colony, for the advantages of complex civilization are better obtained in a city and the joys of a country life, per se, would be better obtained in a hermitage. But the first thing you all need to realize is that social life is more difficult in a colony of comrades than in a village of strangers, still more so than in a city. It requires more tact, more sympathy, more patience and good-will. The chief trouble in almost every colony of radicals is the dogmatic cock-sureness, the critic-ability and combativeness-plus of the members. Almost every member in such a chosen community has a vivid ideal of what life should be in such a place, all mapped and drawn to a scale in his mind, with every body's behavior and belief specified, and he confidently expects to see this at once put in operation on his arrival. But alas, his ideal coincides with that of no one else exactly, for each and every one of his neighbors has a different ideal, also demanding general faith and practice. The result is a clash of intense natures, a Donnybrook Fair of the saints, so to speak, each zealous enthusiast using his plan-of-salvation as a shillelagh to pound his neighbor with. What you must all remember, when you come to a place like this, is that you are all intense individualists and therefore fated to differ, that Harmony is vastly more important than your particular "ism", and that whatever system, plan or method of life finally prevails in the colony will not be exactly what you have imagined, or exactly what anybody else has imagined, but a new and composite thing which the circumstances of the colony and the characters concerned have evolved and which under the friction of all these has proved most fitted to survive. Nothing else than this can be done.

The thing most needed in any colony is a lot of colonists who can live and work harmoniously together and you will find it the hardest thing of all to secure. In fact, if your colony endures it will have to go thru a period of fermentation which will work off and out the unassimilable human units, leaving an effective working majority of those who are comrades in fact as well as in name. If you would assure this harmony you must all set your hearts upon it as your most vital social ideal, the keystone of your social arch without which it will surely fall.

But if Harmony is the keystone of your arch, Liberty and Sympathy are the foundation stones from which it springs. And these must be equal, or it totters. A liberty which would do simply what it pleases is a Sampson which finally pulls down everything and on itself; and a sympathy which does not first grant freedom is worthless indeed. As you are mostly all libertarians I will not go into the theory of liberty, about which many of you know, no doubt, more than myself, but the necessary relation of sympathy to liberty is something which I have found too many libertarians unconscious of or indifferent to. It is all very well to affirm "I will do as I please and take the consequences", if you are willing to take the consequences, but not if you are willing that one of the consequences shall be a successful colony group.

The first step in that liberty which is sympathetic and makes for harmony, as I see it, is that you are willing and glad that other people should be different from yourself in looks, dress, habits, beliefs and ideals, that variation is not only certain but within uninvasive and reasonable limits is exceedingly useful and the thing to be desired to make life interesting and picturesque.

I will quote from some writings of mine on this subject made years ago:

> There are two ways to get liberty. One is for the isolated individual to flee to the savage wilderness, and there, away from his fellows and untrammeled by them, attain such animal liberty as Nature permits. But this, be it noted, is only liberty from man's fulfillment.
>
> The second way is for men to unite and by patiently, faithfully, lovingly cooperating, create for each other, and all, that real liberty which is power over Nature and fullness of self-expression—which is knowledge, which is mastery, which is character; which in the material realm is service, art, leisure and healthful joy.

> Liberty is power.
> And the greatest attainable human liberty will be when men stop struggling for power over each other and all unite for power over Nature.
> To drop men isolated—sink or swim—on little bits of land, is not to give them liberty, leisure, power, home or Nature. All the raw materials are there, but just out of reach. The necessity for constant drudgery of toil from dawn to bed makes all inaccessible.
> But the moment man helps his fellow, power arrives and liberty flowers and art bears fruit. Life on small pieces of land, in individual homes, is ideal, if all one's neighbors are one's helpers and one's liberators, and if to liberate, love and assist is a mutual job. Then combined brain and brawn can progressively lessen the hours of labor, while increasing the product, and power, leisure—real liberty—progressively arrive.

Another quotation is this: "And I would suggest for land-holding groups that they hold land as a corporate body, but in individual allotments, with an understanding that on the withdrawal of any member the title should revert to the group. Otherwise when a member leaves, he might sell his holding to some outsider of absolutely uncongenial traits and so break up the quality of the group."

When a group is formed of people who all know each other and live close together, one great danger is that they will so constantly enter each other's homes and keep up such an intrusive intimacy that privacy will be impossible, and those who love retirement, meditation, quiet literary pursuits, and so on, will find the situation intolerable and at any cost must leave. And such people are usually of the very finest sort, the best material for harmonious cooperation. To lose them would be a grave loss. Yet there are always in every neighborhood, some who have no respect for their own society, but shun it as a vacuum, and rush continually to those about them for refuge from themselves. These become perilous bores unless carefully guarded against. It should be one of your unwritten if not written laws that a member may be as reserved as he likes, a hermit, a very Robinson Crusoe if he pleases, with no reproof from any one. But the mere theory will not be enough, for it is the peculiarity of the bore that he is obtuse and conceited and always imagines that he is the accepted one and his society thrice welcome. You must have some sign or signal, flag, color, emblem, what you will, that can be displayed on the door-post or gate-post and which will be understood as warning all away. And as soon as possible all your homes should be united by telephone so that any really necessary communication can be made without entering the home itself. I would emphasize this point, if you wish to have real liberty.

Many of you, I understand, are communists. Communism is one of the most beautiful of ideals, but in liberty it is only possible between loving friends. The only communism a libertarian can stand for is freedom communism and communism is only free when it is free to refuse. Therefore, it must be based on individualism, on individual possession of property, for communism is sharing and if I possess nothing, I can share nothing, and if I possess nothing, I can refuse nothing. If your communism is forced it destroys your liberty, for liberty is power, the means of power is property. Therefore, your communism and individualism must be reconciled, and both expressed in your colony life. Your communism must be your expression of your sense of solidarity and good will toward each other. Communism cannot be demanded as a right where there is to be liberty—it can only be a gift.

As many of you are city men, unused to country life and its methods, you should employ one or more of your members, if capable, if not then some outsider, to teach and show such of you as may need it the mysteries of gardening, fruit-growing, poultry-raising, also to maintain a model garden where you may learn by example. This may make all the difference between great losses and easy success.

Most men who are fitted for country life, who would make good gardeners and good home-makers are not good businessmen in the modern sense—they are not fitted for the struggles of the market, to buy and sell. You should then choose some trusted member with a talent for this and employ him as your business-agent, to buy for you economically and sell at a profit the things you produce.

The American pioneers did a good deal of practical communism under the name of "bees." When a new man arrived in the community, all came together in a "bee" and rushed up a little home to shelter him, or cleared his land, or plowed it, or whatever might be necessary. You too might do much with the "bee."

I would advise, too, that you mutually insure each other. What

I mean is that in case of sickness you each contribute a few cents a week, whatever the agreed upon sum might be, to the support of the sick member. Or if fire destroys one of your little homes, that you each give five dollars, or whatever you may pledge yourselves for, toward the erection of a new dwelling. These things will bind you all together, make you all feel more secure and your comradeship real.

I take it for granted that most of you would prefer to escape the city altogether and form your abiding place here. To do this you should band your energies upon mutual employment. See if you cannot make your colony a little world in itself, self-supporting, self-sufficient. And by such cooperation and division of labor you can greatly increase your combined efficiency and comfort.

Thus, why should not one of your members do all the baking and perhaps much of the cooking for the whole colony? Why not have a common dining-room where those who chose could get meals without doing their own cooking? Why not have a colony carpenter, a colony barber, a colony cobbler, etc. You should be able to employ a colony tailor and colony seamstress. Of course, no one of these trades or employments might furnish a complete living, but combined with the garden it might make possible a residence permanent in the country, otherwise out of reach.

Many ways besides agriculture might be devised to sell colony products profitably to the outside world also. An arts-and-crafts shop for example. Or one woman instead of gardening might get some tents and furnish them and in summer take boarders from the city, doing their light housekeeping and cooking their meals. These are only hints and pointers.

Self-support and economic freedom should be your goal.

We all want liberty and we should want it. But we must take the universe as it is, for neither you nor I have made it, nor can change its laws. The wise man faces life as it is, and from that basis uses it to serve his purpose. And life as it is is an unstable balance of opposites; opposites that partly conflict, that is, and partly support each other, but are always there and insistent on being included. You can never successfully exclude all of any one and successfully include all of its opposite. It is a waste of time and strength to fight this natural law. In real life you can only have liberty in conjunction with a certain amount of authority and your practical problem, in each new set of circumstances that arises, will be to so reconcile the two that both may serve your benefit. We would fain abolish government because of its abuses, but in some form, government insists on proportionate representation. Josiah Warren saw this and affirmed that in practical action the group must be an individual—which means that somebody's brain must dominate the rest. Tucker saw it and based society on free-contract—but contract is valueless unless there is some power to enforce it on those who treat it as a scrap of paper. Kropotkin saw this and would regulate society by custom, but custom is government—too often the rule of the dead hand—and maybe a very arbitrary and obstructive form of government indeed. The same is true of the boycott. Abolish artificial government and we go back to the primitive struggle and rule of might as right. In some form, and necessarily, the arbitrary and the coercive always emerges. Any way you fix it or leave it alone, when it comes to cooperation or business, you will find yourselves helpless unless you have organization, accepted order and executive power. Apparently, the experience of mankind has evolved nothing so far better for the working reconciliation of liberty and authority than the democratic vote with majority decision; the minority agreeing beforehand to acquiesce.

If you can secure the necessary degree of government thru internal discipline, self-government—self-restraint, loyalty and mutual agreement—well and good. If not, it will have to be accomplished by some degree of external government.

For in your business you will not be able to function without some method of obtaining and enforcing decisions and in your school, you will not have success unless you have an order and discipline—some method, with whatever checks and safeguards, of investing your teachers with sufficient authority to establish a working system out of a chaos of raw materials. Unless you evolve from or implant in your pupils a passionate love of social service and individual efficiency the liberty with which you endow them may be a personal and social curse and your education a failure.

The only true education is that which creates character. For character is the supreme essential of society. This is a truism, a platitude, if you will, but it is a fact we are all too prone to forget or underestimate. There is a certain plan of good intention and comprehending wisdom which some people attain which makes them always and everywhere good neighbors and good citizens. Get enough of such and you are safe. Without such a majority, nothing of theory or brilliant accomplishment can save you. Formulas, philosophies, laws or liberations are all wind and waste, deceptions and disappointments unless the men behind them are men of character.

And if you have the character you will do pretty well no matter what the form or shibboleth.

It is not what men profess, it is what they will and what they do.

There is in almost every human being an instinctive love of beauty though he may be largely unconscious of it or contentious enough to deny it, or unable, by himself, to express it. But if not in his environment he will grow disgusted, pessimistic, heartsick. Order is one of these elements of beauty. Order is everywhere in Nature. All animals lead orderly lives. All "savages," as we call them, have orderly societies and customs of life. Without order social life becomes intolerable and explodes to rearrange on new lines. Whatever its theories of liberty and spontaneity a society must evolve and maintain its own order, or it falls into chaos.

The esthetic is extremely practical. We often regard work as alone practical, but we all work to attain the means of pleasure, and nothing affords us more pleasure than beauty. And the more orderly the work the more efficient. Work beautifully done, to achieve beautiful results, is always the most satisfactory.

But after the work is done, and we are tired and would rest, then disorder and ugliness discourage, dishearten, sicken. If the home to which we go after the day's work is done is not orderly and restfully beautiful the next day's work will be less efficient. Pioneers continually forget or ignore this and, in their concentration on the immediately practical, flout the beautiful until, in dull disgust with the hideousness of their own doings, they sell out and move on. Not until an element arrives which considers order and esthetics does an element which will stick arrive. It would pay any colony, then, that cares to succeed, to see it to that every building, however small or cheap, was made attractive to the eye, and that every bit of ground was laid out or cultivated in such a manner that the relation of it to all others in sight was pleasing, harmonious. For a hundred different people to settle, helter-skelter on a tract of land, all in sight of each other, and proceed without plan, experience or regard to others, to run up every possible type of structure and tear up the earth generally, is very much in total effect on the nerves, as if a hundred would-be musicians seized a hundred instruments of any and every kind and proceeded, each for himself, to scrape, bang and blow, in the confident expectation of creating a symphony.

One of the most practical things any colony could do would be to elect a Committee of Esthetics to give advice to all on matters pertaining to beauty of form, color, line and relation. Make your colony beautiful and your colonists will love it as a home and be happy in it and with each other. Pay no attention to such things and observe the amazing percentage of homesickness, grumbling, quarreling, chronic kicking—the many and frequent secessions and the satire and contempt the whole movement will evoke.

It is simply a scientific fact that any tent, shack or hutch, however cheap or simple, can be made picturesque, and any bit of ground can be made not only productive but a pleasing part of the total landscape.

MALFEW SEKLEW

Sirfessor F. W. Wilkesbarre (aka Malfew Seklew) was born in Great Britain in the 1860s. In the 1890s and early 1900s he was a contributor to and associate editor to *The Eagle and The Serpent*. Sirfessor came to the United States in 1916. He shared an address with Ragnar Redbeard in Chicago in 1927, the year Seklew wrote *The Gospel According to Malfew Seklew*. By the 1930s he was living in New York City. He died in 1938.

> Are you a Simpoleon or a Supercrat? A Peter-pantheist or a Personality? Are you a Bromide or a Sulphide? A nonentity or a reality? Are you an unripe ego or an unfinished organism with underdone understanding and hard boiled beliefs, pingpong principles and petrified prejudices? Do you amble through the atmosphere with the courage of a carrot, the consciousness of a cabbage, the turpitude of a turnip, the pep of a prune, the punch of a parsnip and the psychology of a Sundowner in the swamps of Hobohemia, or do you dash through space with the courage of a Conqueror and the wisdom of a Will-to-Power Man? If not, massage your Mentoids, and be saved—from yourself at your worst.
>
> —Sirfessor F. W. Wilkesbarre,
> *The Gospel According to Malfew Seklew*

Sirfessor Wilkesbarre stands before his tent at the "Talking Marathon" on January 2nd 1929, as part of a photo-op. Printed in the *Vidette-Messenger of Porter County*.

"Seeing the Country in American Fashion." 67
(uncredited) *(1901)*
This find from the *The Shields Daily Gazette of Tyne and Wear* Volume LII Number 14,091 (August 31st, 1901) page 3 is an account of the Laughing (and loafing) Philosopher concurrent his career as a coster, for the Forth (not fourth) fiasco fraught with a policeman fought.

What Shall We Do to Be Saved? 69
Malfew Seklew *(1902)*
Classified advertisement from *The Edinburgh Evening News* for August 23rd 1902.

Malfew Seklew Versus the Watery-Blooded 70
Lucian *(1905)*
The Truthseeker is an atheist periodical established in 1873. *The Freethinker* was a late-comer to atheist periodicals, founded only in 1882. Both are published to this day (but only *The Freethinker* has published the work of Trevor Blake). John W. Gott (1866 – 1922) was sent to prison and sentenced to hard labor for "blasphemy" in England in 1921. John Bruce Glasier (1859 – 1920) was a Scottish socialist later mocked by Sirfessor Malfew Seklew in his 1909 booklet *J. Bruce Glasier / Demi-Gods Demi-Damned, or Halos Hoodooed* (Bradford: J.W. Gott 1909). The Christian Evidence Society was founded in 1870 to defend Christianity from atheist criticism. The identity of Lucian remains as hidden today as the author hoped it would be over a century ago when it appeared in the *Burnley Express* for August 5th 1905.

Nietzsche Again!. 71
Malfew Seklew *(1918)*
A remarkable letter to the editor in *The Truthseeker* Volume 45 Number 49 (December 7 1918) page 773. The laughing philosopher Malfew Seklew as always gives us a full bouquet of literary references. He quotes the 1904 poem "Poland" by Thomas Campbell. He shows himself a reader of the exceptionally rare *Redbeard's Review*, years before Redbeard and Seklew found themselves both at the Dill Pickle Club in Chicago, Illinois. Seklew was an atheist orator, and perhaps reveals some professional jealousy at dismissing fellow heretics Elihu Palmer (1764–1806), Robert Ingersoll (1833–1899) and Voltaire (1694–1778). Mr. C. F. Hunt, of Chicago, mentioned in the article, appears to have been an anti-Georgist. While still in Australia, Arthur Desmond sold copies of Henry George's *Progress and Poverty* through newspaper advertisements.

Portrait of Malfew Seklew 72
(uncredited) *(N.D.)*

Sirfessor "A Commanding Personality" 73
(uncredited) *(1934)*
"New York Day by Day" is an anonymous article from the *Reading Times* (Pennsylvania) Volume 74 Number 264 (January 2, 1934) page 4. The final sentence in this excerpt makes a unique accusation against Sirfessor Malfew Seklew.

Malfew Seklew Bibliography. 74
Trevor Blake *(2019)*
Works by, about or mentioning Sirfessor Malfew Seklew.

"Seeing the Country in American Fashion." Unsympathetic Police Object.
(Uncredited) (1901)

Malfew Seklew, who describes himself as "an alien, seeing the country in the American fashion," was summoned before the Newcastle Bench, yesterday, on charges of obstruction, the first in Forth Street, on the 16th inst., and the second West Clayton Street, on the 21st inst.

The officer, in the first case, informed the Bench about 7:50 p.m. defendant was standing on a chair in Forth Street, lecturing to a crowd, which extended from one side the street to the other. He refused to desist or give his name, and used foul language. The constable therefore took to him the Westgate Station, defendant resisting all the way.

Sir Charles Hammond, the presiding magistrate, asked whether defendant was using foul language when on the chair, or whether reserved for the police. The officer replied: For the police.

Defendant: Did I call you a loafer—Yes.—Is that foul language?—The Clerk (Mr. Roberts): He was in his policeman's uniform.—Proceeding, defendant said he was on "common property,"—the land was in Chancery and did not belong to the police.—Sir Charles: The police have as much control over property in Chancery as you have over your hat when it is on your head.—This intimation seemed rather to surprise the defendant.

Another officer deposed to having cautioned defendant shortly before the previous witness spoke to him. At that time he was selling a patent tie maker.—Defendant: I protest. That is not relevant.—The Clerk: It very relevant, I think, as showing your object and intention.

Addressing the Bench, defendant first made allegations of brutality against the police, and went on to say that he was "an alien seeing the country in the American fashion." He was earning his living selling a little patent of his own, and at the same time he was lecturing on egoism, individualism, and various other philosophies.—Sir Charles: "Where do you lecture?"—"In the street."

"On this occasion," defendant added seriously, "I was lecturing in a place which I understand has been used for 20 years, without police interference. I was preaching my philosophy to the English people—a brand new philosophy. (Laughter.) In fact was doing what Jesus is supposed to have done, I was talking the masses."

The Chief Constable proved a conviction against the defendant for using obscene language at Nottingham in October last year. That, Seklew explained, was "a put up job, the same as this."

A fine of 40s and costs was imposed, with the alternative of one month.

The second case was gone into, the officer who proved it, stating that when he spoke to defendant, he appealed to the crowd, mostly composed of youths under 20 years, "to resist, as free born citizens of Newcastle, the aggression of the police." (Laughter.)—Another fine of 40s and costs with a similar alternative, was imposed.

What Shall We Do to Be Saved?
Malfew Seklew   (1902)

Classified advertisement from the Edinburgh Evening News for August 23rd 1902. "The Mound" is an artificial hill made between 1781 and 1830 in Edinburgh, Scotland, between New Town and Old Town. It is suggested by the Union of Egoists that in 1902 Sirfessor Seklew (then in his early 40s) had been to and returned from Chicago, U.S.A. The term "atheogist" may be one of the many coined by Sirfessor Seklew.

> MALFEW SEKLEW, Atheogist, from Chicago, U.S.A., will LECTURE at the MOUND, SUNDAY, 2.45 and 6.45 p.m.
> Subject—"What Shall we do to be Saved."
> Opposition invited.

MALFEW SEKLEW, Atheogist, from Chicago, U.S.A., will LECTURE at the MOUND, SUNDAY, 2:40 and 6:45 p.m.
Subject—"What Shall we do to be Saved."
Opposition invited.

Malfew Seklew Versus the Watery-Blooded Lucian (1905)

Dear Sir,

Of the many letters published in this column during the past fortnight treating of the *Truthseeker* and blasphemy, none have. I think, made a candid examination of that paper. *The Truthseeker*, though has "fought good fight" against the ancient blasphemy laws, is largely boycotted by tolerant Rationalists: the *Literary Guide* speaks of "Gott and his wild associates"; the *Freethinker* practically ignores them. Anyone refusing to accept the anti-Christian-plus-Malthusian cordial of the *Truthseeker* is denounced in language which is neither decent, courteous, nor manly. For instance, I have now before me a copy containing an article signed "Malfew Seklew." This unknown scribe refers to large-hearted Bruce Glasier as "a watery-blooded weak imitation of the weeping Nazarene." Christian Evidence men the paper refers to as those "whose brains are surely fit to be boiled down to billstickers' paste." The same issue includes a letter ending thus: "Socialism will never have the ghost of a chance until the fat-headed followers of creeping Jesus have got the rhinoceros-like scales scraped out of their blubbering eyes. Send me two of your bedding parcels, for which I enclose cheque."

This in a paper professedly devoted to mental freedom and social progress! I have quoted sufficient. I hold no brief for Bruce Glasier; I am no admirer of Christian Evidence lecturers; I hold unorthodox opinions concerning Jesus of Nazareth; I smile at allegations of blasphemy, at pedants who burn literature because it disagrees with them; I like occasionally words that bite, that irritate—such are often needed; but neither I nor any other Rationalist can defend such scurrilous and miserable attacks of the type I have quoted: attacks not on principle but on individuals. I am sure that all earnest students—religious or secular, reformists or revolutionists—must depreciate such passages; they are a blight on Freethought, and a blur on our press.

Yours truly,
LUCIAN

NIETZSCHE AGAIN!
MALFEW SEKLEW (1918)

To the Editor of *The Truth Seeker*:

I am enclosing you a clipping from a London radical Journal (*Redbeard's Review*). It is very evidently the article on Nietzsche which has made Mr. C. F. Hunt, Chicago, so awfully mad.

Nietzsche, I may be allowed to point out, was of Polish blood and Polish descent. He was the same breed and race as Kosciusko. Campbell the poet says: "And freedom shrieked as Kosciusko fell."

Nietzsche's family were all strongly involved in libertarian ideas. They were driven out of Poland by intolerant Catholics because they upheld the Freethinkers of private judgment in religious matters. Furthermore, Friedrich Nietzsche in his writings (all translated into English) destroyed German imperialism more fiercely than any American editor has ever done. Nietzsche is very much misunderstood. I think if Mr. C. F. Hunt would read Nietzsche it would do him good. Nietzsche was an excellent Freethinker, an atheist, and goes far beyond Palmer, Ingersoll or Voltaire, in his ferocious assaults upon Christianity, its advocates and its defenders. His Anti-Christ is splendid. In my opinion the article to which I allude is in no sense whatever pro-German. Might I also point out to Mr. Hunt that all good Americans profit substantially by the wars of the past. These wars (waged for hundreds of years against French, English, Spaniards, Indians, and Americans) have given us the lands to which we are now erecting our glorious democracy.

Portrait of Malfew Seklew
(uncredited) *(n.d.)*

Malfew Seklew.
"The Man without a Soul."

Sirfessor "A Commanding Personality"
(uncredited) *(1934)*

Of course there's a good deal of substance to the old bromide about newspapermen meeting a lot of interesting people. A lot of highly unusual people, too, with novel missions in life. There is Mr. F. M. Wilkesbarr, for example, who goes about lecturing on neo-determinism. A commanding personality, he announces that he is from the Institute of Supermanity, England, and is president of the Society of Social Supercrats. He tells people that "the molecule of mirth has set out to murder the microbe of misery, while the memboid of energy gazes upon the sightly scene with ecstasy and eclat." Mr. Wilkesbarr does very well, financially, with his lecturing.

Malfew Seklew Bibliography
Trevor Blake (2019)

"30 in Talkfest Gab Away for Prize of $1,000." *St. Louis Star and Times, The*. December 26, 1928.

A Constant Reader. "Advice to Allen." *Day Book, The*, November 24, 1916.

"Altruism Is a Fundamental Principle of Nature." *Day Book, The*, April 1, 1916.

Anonymous, ed. *Enemies of Society / An Anthology of Individualist & Egoist Thought*. Ardent Press, 2011.

Bailey, Redwood. "Definitions." *Day Book, The*, February 5, 1916.

"Books Received." *To-Morrow*, February 1908.

"Broadcasting." *Sheffield Daily Telegraph*, December 8, 1923.

"Broadcasting." *Derby Daily Telegraph*, December 8, 1923.

"Broadcasting." *Derby Daily Telegraph*, January 12, 1924.

"Broadcasting." *Sheffield Daily Telegraph*, January 23, 1924.

"Broadcasting." *Derby Daily Telegraph*, January 23, 1924.

"Broadcasting." *Sheffield Daily Telegraph*, January 30, 1924.

"Broadcasting." *Derby Daily Telegraph*, January 30, 1924.

"Broadcasting." *Derby Daily Telegraph*, February 8, 1924.

"Broadcasting." *Sheffield Daily Telegraph*, February 8, 1924.

"Broadcasting." *Derby Daily Telegraph*, February 27, 1924.

"Broadcasting." *Derby Daily Telegraph*, March 25, 1924.

"Broadcasting." *Sheffield Daily Telegraph*, March 25, 1924.

"Broadcasting." *Sheffield Daily Telegraph*. March 27, 1924.

"Broadcasting." *Gloucester Citizen*, May 29, 1924.

"Broadcasting." *Sheffield Daily Telegraph*. May 29, 1924.

"Broadcasting." *Derby Daily Telegraph*, May 29, 1924.

"Broadcasting To-Day." *Western Daily Press*, January 12, 1924.

"Broadcasting To-Day." *Western Daily Press*, January 23, 1924.

"Broadcasting To-Day." *Western Daily Press*, January 30, 1924.

"Broadcasting To-Day." *Western Daily Press*, February 9, 1924.

"Broadcasting To-Day." *Western Daily Press*, February 27, 1924.

"Broadcasting To-Day." *Western Daily Press*, March 25, 1924.

"Broadcasting To-Day." *Western Daily Press*, May 24, 1924.

"Celtic Ancestry." *Western Mail*. December 1, 1944.

"Church Notices." *Edinburg Evening News*. August 23, 1902.

"Coasters Union, The." *Kentish Independent*, July 29, 1904.

Conder, Darrell. *I Beheld Desmond as Lightning Fall - To Chicago!* Port Townsend: eLudic Domain, 2007.

"Day to Day / Coincidence." *Nottingham Journal*, March 2, 1938.

"Do You Know What a Stuffed Club Is?" *Little Journeys to Homes of Great Lovers* XIX, no. 6 (December 1906).

Double X. "These Propositions." *Day Book, The*, February 11, 1916.

Druck, Sam. "Nietzsche." *Day Book, The*, February 22, 1916.

Emmanuel, Alexandra. "Literary Reception of Nietzschean Ideas in Relation to Selected Works of Modernist Literature, The." University of Leeds, 2010.

"F. M. Wilkes-Barre Quits Talkfest, 24 Still Remain." *Wilkes-Barre Times Leader, The Evening News*. December 28, 1928.

Fisher, S. "What Our Readers Think / Recollections of a Remarkable Nottingham Character." *Nottingham Journal*. March 3, 1938.

"For Listeners." *Sheffield Independent*, December 8, 1923.

"Forty Years on a Soap Box." *New York Evening Post*. April 15, 1930.

"Is Socialism Desirable?" *Day Book, The*, November 25, 1916.

J. S. "Coined Words." *Day Book, The*, February 16, 1916.

John Crerar Library, The / Twenty-Second Annual Report for the Year 1916. Chicago: Board of Directors, 1917.

"Karl Marx vs. Malfew Seklew; Which Is the Better System of Philosophy?" *Day Book, The*, April 8, 1916.

Kentrick, John F. "Answers 'Just a Girl,'" February 14, 1916.

Kibbler, W. "Got Kibbler's Goat." *Day Book, The*, January 21, 1916.

———. "He Hit the Nail." *Day Book, The*, November 24, 1916.

———. "IWW, The." *Day Book, The*, October 5, 1916.

———. "Kibbler Kids Kend'r'k." *Day Book, The*, March 11, 1916.

———. "Of Men." *Day Book, The*, February 26, 1916.

———. "Steven Is Popular." *Day Book, The*, November 18, 1916.

———. "Stomach Pads." *Day Book, The*, February 21, 1916.

———. "Who Can Answer?" *Day Book, The*, October 28, 1916.

Kibbler, Wm. "Wilkesbarre." *Day Book, The*, March 9, 1916.

Kilgallen, James L. "Marathon 'Gabfest' Opens in New York, Requires Good Lungs," December 26, 1928.

———. "Nut Marathon Now Underway." *Marysville Journal-Tribune*. December 26, 1928.

Krummel, Richard Frank, and Evelyn S. Krummel. *Nietzsche und der deutsche Geist / Ausbreitung und Wirkung des Nietzscheschen*

Werkes im deutschen Sprachraum bis zum Ende. Berlin: De Gruyter, 2006.

Kuhn, Irene. "Hobo Gives Ego Handout." *Daily News*. November 11, 1928.

Leibson, Art. "Some Characters You Just Never Will Forget." *El Paso Times*. December 23, 1990, Main Edition edition.

———. "Unique Character Englightened Store's Patrons." *El Paso Times*. July 27, 1986, Main Edition edition.

Levish, Thomas. "Preparedness." *Day Book, The*, February 15, 1916.

Lewis, W. J. "Children a Luxury." *Day Book, The*, January 28, 1916.

Longa, Ernesto A. *Anarchist Periodicals in English Published in the United States: (1833–1955) / an Annotated Guide*. Lanham: Scarecrow Press, 2010.

Love, Sam. "Gabble Grind Weakens One." *San Bernadino Sun*. December 27, 1928.

Lucien, and Malfew Seklew. "Bradford Truthseekers, The." *Burnley Express*, August 5, 1905.

Martindale, C. C. "Lion in Daniel's Den, The." *Month, The*, n.d.

"Miscellaneous." *Daily Herald*, June 13, 1914.

"Miscellaneous." *Daily Herald*, June 15, 1914.

"Miscellaneous." *Daily Herald*, June 17, 1914.

Nash, David. *Blasphemy in Modern Britain / 1789 to the Present*. Aldershot: Ashgate, 1999.

"New York Day by Day." *Reading Times*. January 2, 1934.

Niver, Joseph, ed. *Earth: A History / Together with a Facsimile of Earth and Selected Letters of Romain Rolland and Leo Tolstoy*. Millwood: KTO Press, 1977.

"Nut Marathon Now Underway." *Marysville Journal-Tribune*. December 26, 1928.

"Our Bill." "Panic." *Day Book, The*, February 17, 1916.

Pack, Ernest. *Trial and Imprisonment of J. W. Gott for Blasphemy, The*. Bradford: Freethought Socialist League, n.d.

Plotkin, Harry. "Everybody's Business." *Day Book, The*, March 11, 1916.

"Poetic Beer Drinker, A." *Express and Telegraph*. February 3, 1920.

Preston, M. R. "Hard Words." *Day Book, The*, February 16, 1916.

"Programme For To-Day." *Northern Whig*, March 25, 1924.

"Publications Received." *Blue-Grass Blade*. February 9, 1908.

Rasmussen, M. "Who Can This Be?" *Day Book, The*, February 27, 1916.

"Resolved, That Ignorance Is More Beneficial to the Race than Knowledge." *Day Book, The*, January 2, 1917.

"Resolved, That Ignorance Is More Beneficial to the Race than Knowledge." *Day Book, The*, January 6, 1917.

"Resolved: That Malfew Seklew Solves All Problems of Life." *Day Book, The*, December 1, 1916.

Royle, Edward. *Radicals, Secularists, and Republicans: Popular Freethought in Britain, 1866-1915*. Manchester: Manchester University Press, 1980.

"Runs Out of Words, Put Out of Contest." *New York Times*. December 27, 1928.

S., M. "Surfessor of Egoism." *Guardian, The*. September 25, 1934.

Sakolsky, Ron, ed. *Surrealist Subversions / Rants, Writings & Images by the Surrealist Movement in the United States*. New York: Autonomedia, 2003.

Schilling, N. J. "Socialism Wrong." *Day Book, The*, February 9, 1916.

Schilling, W. J. "Altruism." *Day Book, The*, February 19, 1916.

———. "Knocks Socialism." *Day Book, The*, January 27, 1916.

Seklew, Malfew. "Agency Vacant Quick Selling Line." *Whitstable Times and Herne Bay Herald*, March 14, 1914.

———. "Celui Qui Est..." *La Gazette de Chateau-Gontier*, October 1, 1933.

———. "For Sale." *Daily Herald*, March 21, 1914.

———. "For Sale." *Daily Herald*, March 25, 1914.

———. "For Sale." *Daily Herald*, March 26, 1914.

———. "For Sale." *Daily Herald*, March 28, 1914.

———. *Gospel According to Malfew Seklew, The*. Chicago: Spencella and Winsex, 1927.

———. *Gospel According to Malfew Seklew, The / a Revelation of Revaluations*. Chicago: F. M. Wilkesbarr, 1927.

———. "Housewives!" *Western Chronicle*, November 27, 1908.

———. "Housewives." *Western Chronicle*, December 4, 1908.

———. *J. Bruce Glasier / Demi-Gods Demi-Damned, or Halo's Hoodoo'd*. Bradford: J. W. Gott, 1909.

———. "Malfew Seklew." *Edinburgh Evening News*, August 23, 1902.

———. "Miscellaneous." *Daily Herald*, March 14, 1914.

———. "Miscellaneous." *Daily Herald*, April 8, 1914.

———. "Miscellaneous." *Daily Herald*, April 20, 1914.

———. "Miscellaneous." *Daily Herald*, April 21, 1914.

———. "Miscellaneous." *Daily Herald*, April 23, 1914.
———. "Miscellaneous." *Daily Herald*, May 2, 1914.
———. "Miscellaneous." *Daily Herald*, May 4, 1914.
———. "Miscellaneous." *Daily Herald*, May 5, 1914.
———. "Nietzsche Again!" *Truthseeker, The* 45, no. 49 (December 7, 1918): 773.
———. "Novelties." *Daily Herald*, June 16, 1914.
———. "Prepaid Advertisements." *Daily Herald*, March 20, 1914.
———. "Publications, Etc." *Daily Herald*, March 27, 1914.
———. "Rare and Choice Books for Sale." *Whitstable Times and Herne Bay Herald*, March 21, 1914.
———. "Rejection of Christianity." *People's Press, The* 12, no. 39 (December 11, 1909).
———. "Seeing the Country in American Fashion." *Shields Daily Gazette*, August 31, 1901.
———. "Situations Vacant." *Western Chronicle*, April 3, 1914.
———. "Stable to Let." *Whitstable Times and Herne Bay Herald*, March 21, 1914.
———. "To the Bradford Daily Telegraph." *Bradford Daily Telegraph*, February 28, 1903.
Seklew, Malfew, and Spencella Maljean. *Victor Grayson, M. P. / A Rhapsody on a Reality*, 1909.
Seklew, Malfew, and J. R. Lloyd Thomas. "Celtic Ancestry." *Western Mail*, December 1, 1944.
"Seven Quit Talking Match." *New York Times*. December 28, 1928.
"Seven Wonders of the Ego, The." *Day Book, The*, March 17, 1916.
"Sirfessor of 'Wireless' Fame, The." *Guardian, The*. April 5, 1924.
"Sirfessor of 'Wireless' Fame, The." *Guardian, The*. April 8, 1924.
"Sirfessor Wilkesbarre and B. Lester Weber Will Debate." *Day Book, The*, February 26, 1916.
"Sirfessor Wilkesbarre. Debate: 'Egoism vs. Socialism.'" *Day Book, The*, March 11, 1916.
"Sirfessor Wilkesbarre Lectures on the Ego and His Own at Hobo College." *Day Book, The*, April 12, 1917.
"Sirfessor Wilkesbarre Lectures Society of Social Aristocrats, 'From Simpoleon to Superman.'" *Day Book, The*, January 29, 1916.
"Sirfessor Wilkesbarre Speaks: 'Socialism a Brain Disease.'" *Day Book, The*, February 19, 1916.
"Sirfessor Wilkesbarre Will Lecture / Can Socialism Save the People."

Day Book, The, March 9, 1916.

"Sirfessor Wilkesbarre Will Lecture on 'Altruism, an Enemy of the People.'" *Day Book, The*, February 12, 1916.

"Sirfessor Wilkesbarre Will Open Class on How to Be a Superman, and the Evolution of the Ego." *Day Book, The*, March 2, 1916.

"Sirfessor Wilkesbarre Will Speak on 'Birth Control.'" *Day Book, The*, January 13, 1917.

"Sirfessor Wilkesbarre Will Start Class for Study of Supermanism, for Men and Women." *Day Book, The*, March 7, 1916.

"Sirfessor Wilkesbarre's Class." *Day Book, The*, February 24, 1916.

Slaughter, Kevin I, ed. *Bible Not Borrowed from the Neighbors, A / Essays & Aphorisms on Egoism*. Baltimore: Underworld Amusements, 2013.

Sloan, R. H. "Sirfessor's Satire." *Day Book, The*, February 11, 1916.

Smith, Frank. "Growing." *Day Book, The*, February 24, 1916.

"Soap Box King." *Yorkshire Evening Post*. February 25, 1938.

"Soap Box King / Well-Known Agitator Dies in New York." *Yorkshire Evening Post*. February 24, 1938.

"Soap-Box King, 77, Dies in Bellevue." *New York Times*. February 10, 1938.

"Socialism / Negative: Sirfessor Wilkesbarre." *Day Book, The*, December 1, 1916.

"Society of Social Aristocrats." *Chicago Tribune*. January 29, 1916.

"Society of Social Aristocrats." *Chicago Tribune*. February 12, 1916.

Steven, Allen. "Divorce Cure, A." *Day Book, The*, February 16, 1917.

———. "How to Stop Murder." *Day Book, The*, January 25, 1917.

———. "To Bess H." *Day Book, The*, July 10, 1916.

"Sunday Lecture Notices, Etc." *Freethinker, The*, December 11, 1898, 798.

"Super-Socialism, The." *Day Book, The*, March 4, 1916.

Sweeny, E. "Love." *Day Book, The*, March 4, 1916.

Sweetland, D. F. "Too Much Ego." *Day Book, The*, April 8, 1916.

T. T. "Sirfessor's Pedigree." *Day Book, The*, February 26, 1916.

"The Truth Seeker." *The Truth Seeker.*, 1894.

Thompson, Bonar. *Hyde Park Orator*. New York: G.P. Putnam's Sons, 1934.

"To-Day's Broadcasting." *Gloucestershire Echo*, December 8, 1923.

"To-Day's Broadcasting." *Gloucestershire Echo*, January 30, 1924.

"To-Day's Broadcasting." *Gloucestershire Echo*, February 16, 1924.

"To-Day's Broadcasting." *Gloucestershire Echo*, March 25, 1924.
"To-Day's Broadcasting." *Gloucestershire Echo*, May 29, 1924.
"To-Days Broadcasting Programmes." *Nottingham Journal*, March 25, 1924.
"To-Day's Programme." *Leeds Mercury*, February 16, 1924.
"Tom-Cat Vibrators, 'Hamlets,' and Ordinary 'Reds.'" *Literary Digest*, July 17, 1920.
"To-Night's Broadcasting." *Nottingham Evening Post*, January 30, 1924.
Trial and Imprisonment of J. W. Gott for Blasphemy. Bradford: Freethought Socialist League, 1911.
"W. K." "No Quibler." *Day Book, The*, February 12, 1916.
"Wanted a Leader." *NZ Truth*, December 2, 1916.
"WGBS 5:45 The Sirfessor Speaks." *New York Times*. April 4, 1931.
Wilkes, Fred, Trevor Blake. *Gospel According to Malfew Seklew: And Other Writings By and About Sirfessor Wilkesbarre, The*. Edited by Kevin I. Slaughter. Underworld Amusements, 2014.
Wilkesbarre, F. M. "Answer to a Symposium, An." *Eagle and the Serpent, The*, February 1927.
———. "Individualism and Socialism / A Contrast." *Eagle and the Serpent, The*, February 1927.
Wilkesbarre, Sirfessor. "Simple Words from Sirfessor." *Day Book, The*, February 10, 1916.
———. "Sirfessor Replies." *Day Book, The*, January 28, 1916.
"Wireless." *Leeds Mercury*, January 30, 1924.
"Wireless Age, The." *Hull Daily Mail*, January 30, 1924.
"Worlds Remade While You Wait - on the East Side." *New York Tribune*. January 26, 1919.

LAURANCE LABADIE

Laurance Labadie (1898 – 1975) was an individualist anarchist with a strong appreciation for the egoism of Max Stirner. As a teenager, Laurance published a journal titled The Whippo-wil. As a young man in the 1930s he wrote hundreds of essays on individual anarchism, economics, religion and more. Labadie was a correspondent and colleague to Benjamin R. Tucker and Steven T. Byington, the publisher and editor of The Ego and His Own (1907 edition); to J. Wm. Lloyd (see elsewhere in this issue of Der Geist); Mildred J. Loomis (of Ralph Borsodi's School of Living); and S. E. Parker (source of the egoist Sydney E. Parker Archive at sidparker.com).

> There are not very many people who can intelligently understand Stirner. The reason is the "Judeo-Christian ethic" which dominates the viewpoints of people in the western hemisphere. They are nothing if not moralists. Whereas Stirner is primarily an amoralist. [...] What goes into one man's stomach does not nourish another man, and in a circumstance of absolute scarcity morality goes by the board. Men's interests conflict and a scramble results. It is inherent in the situation, and Christians and communists, moralists both, are confronted with a situation wherein their nicely-spun "commandments" go fluttering in the breeze.
>
> —Laurance Labadie, *Anarcho-Pessimism*

Group photo of five men. Laurance Labadie is 2nd from right (circa 1960s). Care of the Labadie Photograph Collection, University of Michigan.

To Butt, or Not to Butt. 83
Laurance Labadie   (1958)
Written December 18, 1958. From "Laurance Labadie / Miscellaneous Writings Volume 2" as compiled by John Zube in 2001. Just one of tens of thousands of rare individualist, egoist and other heretical texts archived by the Union of Egoists at The Libertarian Microfiche Project (LibertarianMicrofiche.com).

In a Pickle!. 84
Laurance Labadie   (1965)
Laurance Labadie (1898 – 1975) was an individualist anarchist, influenced by the work of his father Jo Labadie, Benjamin R. Tucker, Max Stirner and Ragnar Redbeard. He was affiliated with the School of Living, but because of his confrontational nature he was also a harsh critic of the group. "In a Pickle!" was written January 29th, 1965 From "Laurance Labadie / Miscellaneous Writings Volume 12" as compiled by John Zube in 2001

Laurance Labadie on Max Stirner's Economic Views 85
Laurance Labadie   (1966)
Footnotes by John Zube   (2001)
Another text the Libertarian Microfiche Project, with footnotes dated 6.9.01 from John Zube.

E. Armand, "Freedom" and the H-Bomb. 86
S.E. Parker, Laurance Labadie   (1962)
An exchange between two egoist researchers on the past and the present, published here for the first time. S. E. Parker (1929 - 2012) was an occasional writer for the anarchist periodical *Freedom*, with a special interest in the individualist tradition of anarchism. Parker and Labadie were friendly critics of *Freedom*, having 'grown up' with it. *Balanced Living* was the periodical of back-to-the-land pioneers, the School of Living, founded by Ralph Borsodi (1886 - 1977). The Union of Egoists is in possession of the remaining stock of literature published by the School of Living. Man! was the title from 1901 to 1944 of a magazine begun in 1870 as The Journal of Anthropology and ended in 2012 as The Journal of the Royal Anthropological Institute. Slaves to Duty by John Badcock was published by Benjamin R. Tucker (1894) and again by Laurance Labadie (1938); the Union of Egoists has published *For Love and Money* by Badcock (writing as Leighton Pagan) in 2016. Victor Yarros (1865 - 1956) was a contributor to Tucker's newspaper *Liberty* and law-office-partner to "Scopes Monkey Trial" lawyer Clarence Darrow.

To Butt, or Not to Butt
Laurance Labadie (1958)

At some time in the distant past, no date given, some fellow bending over was given a boot in the britches. To some this appeared such a delightful spectacle that they made a game of it. Soon the game spread all over the world.

In later times some fellow who did the booting started wearing a brown shirt. This was quite an innovation and caused considerable comment. Later another wore a red shirt.

Heretofore conversation was sprinkled with whether one had had his boot in the pants this week, or no. But later the discussion hinged around whether the booter should wear a brown or a red shirt. Some even hinted darkly of other colors. Still later the discussions became arguments, and in time the battles became hot and bloody.

Learned men wrote treatises about how, when, and where the populaces should get their boots in the britches. Who was to do the booting, and on what days; whether the first of the week or at the end, and numerous other details. Then, too, they waxed wroth over what to call the booting game. Some said it should be called democracy. Others said no, it should be called people's democracy, and as the arguments proceeded other names cropped in. Some believed in national rump kicking; while others said that was foolish, there should be an international rump kicking organization. And the arguments went on and on.

At one of the great conclaves trying to work out a satisfactory system of rules for rump kicking, involving compromise, checks and balances, and a great deal of other complicated matters involved, I saw a fellow on the sidelines feeling his butt—and scratching his head.

IN A PICKLE!
LAURANCE LABADIE (1965)

I don't know of any party, sect, or movement with whom I couldn't be ascribed to, not by those in any particular group, but by their rivals. In the same sense, I could not be identified with any group - a non-labeling which fits me precisely. I am indeed a "minority of one," and I prefer it that way inasmuch as I do not wish to be associated with any of the lunacies I see about me.

But as an independent, an alienated and non-involved person, who presumably for that reason might be considered more able to see things objectively than most people; a person who moreover sees the course of human events in an almost fatalistic light - what the hell should I have to offer except pessimism and almost non-action in the face of inevitable cataclysm?

"You are not uninvolved," they may say. "You suffer a certain amount of miseries, and are going to be snuffed out like the rest." "Your disinterestedness and unconcern are a pose. It is only a mask for your inertia and lack of courage." Well, I could not deny this.

But I can say this: Inasmuch as my own ideas are not only contrary and inimical to the powers-that-be, who wouldn't hesitate a moment to snuff me out, they are likewise contrary and inimical to all the movements and sects and parties that I know anything about. And I damn well know, by the flavor of their advocacies, that they wouldn't have any less scruples in seeing me effectively urged into the ash barrel, if indeed they wouldn't help with the heave-to, than the members and supporters of The Establishment.

So, you bastards' categorizing of me as a cowardly dud in effect means that you'd prefer for me to stick my neck out so that you could lop my head off. You're damn well right, I am involved. I have a personal interest at stake. And that interest includes such impulses of self-preservation as to deprive you all from cutting my precious throat. I have been around long enough to exude whatever part of my gullibility about the considerateness of "human nature" as to believe that a recalcitrant to any of the schemes of world-fixing so ardently favored by this or the other of the fixers bent to *do me good* means other than haste in having me see my maker.

Fuck you!

Laurance Labadie on Max Stirner's Economic Views
Laurance Labadie (1966)
***John Zube*, footnotes** (2001)

I cannot now remember and furnish the reference, but I have read somewhere that Stirner translated Adam Smith's *Wealth of Nations* into German. There is little or no question that he realized that for a "free economy" to work satisfactorily, it was positively necessary that competition be given the largest scope of operation. Which means that opportunity to produce and exchange needed to be equitable. In other words, it demanded an equitable access to land.[1] He certainly understood that opportunities to exchange products without being held up by financial monopolies was also an essential prerequisite.[2]

That he did not make an elaborate economic analysis of economics in his *Ego and His Own* does not warrant the belief that he was unaware or ignorant of economics. The main purpose of his book was to show up the fatuousness of the self-styled revolutionaries of his time, when they thought, believed, or hoped that any sort of revolution or insurrection could be satisfactorily carried out by other than self-acknowledged egoists who understood what they were about. His target obviously was communists—whom he no doubt considered fools fighting for their own enslavement.[3]

---

1   I rather believe that especially here he would have upheld the supposed "right of the strongest," which in most cases is the existing statist land title system, rather than free competition with it, by various other land reform "ideals," all at the expense and risk of their supporters.

2   Just like L.L., he was insufficiently specific about the details of monetary and financial freedom. The strength of Ulrich von Beckerath's writings on the subject lies in the details and his avoidance and refutations of popular errors, myths and prejudices in this field, shared by most monetary reformers, even most of those who advocated degrees of monetary freedom.

3   Marx felt this attack and tried to defend himself by a long and sharp counter-attack, which is largely said to reveal the flaws in Marx's thinking. I have not yet bothered to microfiche this book by Marx's, since all too much literature, with its pro and con, has already been dedicated to Marxism and anti-Marxism. The sooner most of the ideas, that he scrounged together and turned into a "system," become altogether forgotten, as long refuted errors myths and prejudices, the better.—Perhaps only in an Encyclopaedia of the Best Refutations should they be "preserved," so that others do not too easily fall for these notions, once again.

E. Armand, "Freedom" and the H-Bomb
S.E. Parker, Laurance Labadie (1962)

May 16, 1962.
Dear Mr. Labadie,

I am engaged in the project of translating and publishing the works of E. Armand and other anarchist individualist writers. Several articles have already appeared in *Freedom* and two items have been published separately (I enclose copies of these). However, I am in need of help in the shape of translations and I am wondering if you would be willing to translate, or if you know of anyone else who would be so. Financial help would also be welcome.

During the last year I have been receiving *Balanced Living* and have noticed your name mentioned in its columns. I have noticed also that you have written a pamphlet on "Government and H-Bombs." Is this still available? If it is, I would be willing to review it in *Freedom*, as I have done two pamphlets by Don Werkheiser. Are any other of your writings available? (The late E. Armand sent me some of your leaflets.)

I look forward to hearing from you.

Sincerely,
S.E. Parker.

∉

Dear Mr. S. E. Parker

In reply to your letter of May 16: I am familiar only with the English language; and I am not acquainted with anyone available for translations from French. Enclosed is a mimeographed copy of the article you request. Since I live practically a hermit's life, I am not in much contact with radicals. However, I have written quite a bit during these last years, possibly very little of it publishable, or at least it hasn't been. It is rather pessimistic stuff, since it appears to me that the prospects for liberty are almost hopeless.

The *Freedom* (London) people have kindly sent me their paper for a good many years, and lately I have been able to reimburse them. I have read it religiously, and suppose that one way to give my opinion of this journal would be to say that I consider it about 90% communist and 10% anarchist.

I have a very dim view of the deleterious effect which "communist anarchism" has had on the genuine article.

The ignorant "replies" which have been made to some of your letters is indicative. And yet, amid the welter of idiocy regarding the current scene, I tend to favor them.

Sincerely
Laurance Labadie
20 De Baun Lane, Suffern, N.Y.

∉

20.6.62.
Dear Friend,
    Many thanks for your letter and the enclosures.

I think that, rather than try to summarize the article on atomic war in a review, it would be far better to send it to *Freedom* for publication in its columns and, with your permission, I shall do this.

I agree, in the main, with your estimation of *Freedom*.

In spite of their "communist" bias, however, its editors are willing to publish other anarchist points of view—something which, I am told, certain other anarchist journals—e.g. in Italy, are not prepared to do. Having "grown up with *F*" and, in spite of our now divergent interpretations of anarchism, still remaining on friendly terms with its editors I am particularly glad they maintain such an open attitude.

You may be interested to know that among the items sent to me by the companion of the late E. Armand—was a Spanish translation of one of your essays called "Is Communism Practical?" Also a small booklet of essays by your father and some of his verses. (I have also acquired, from other sources, copies of *Man!* containing your "Reflections on Liberty" and other articles, and also Tucker's *Why I Am an Anarchist* and Badcock's *Slaves to Duty* published by you.)

I have just read again James J. Martin: *Men Against the State*. In it I found references to Victor Yarros' rejection of anarchism and Tuckers repudiation of him in letters to you. However, in one of the few copies of *L'Unique* I possess there is an article by Yarros (circa 1948, I think) which seems—as far as my extremely fragmentary French allows me to judge—to be quite sympathetic to anarchist individualism. Have you any idea where he now stands?

I note from your letter that you live at Suffern. This was, I believe, the address of the School of Living before it moved to Brookvale, Ohio. Does any trace of it remain in Suffern? (I was surprised to find —when I came across *Balanced Living* last year—that such a distinct anarchist trend has emerged from the muddled idealism of Borsodi.)

With best wishes,
S.E. Parker.

MAX STIRNER / *THE EGO AND HIS OWN*

Max Stirner (October 25, 1806–June 26, 1856) was a German philosopher. He is often seen as one of the forerunners of nihilism, existentialism, postmodernism, and anarchism, especially of individualist anarchism. Stirner's main work is *The Ego and His Own* (*Der Einzige und sein Eigentum*). This book is the wellspring of egoism. *Der Einzige* was first published in 1845 in Leipzig, and has since appeared in numerous editions and translations.

> I write because I wish to make for ideas, which are my ideas, a place in the world. If I could foresee that these ideas must take from you peace of mind and repose, if in these ideas that I sow I should see the germs of bloody wars and even the cause of the ruins of many generations, I would nevertheless continue to spread them. It is neither for the love of you nor even for the love of truth that I express what I think. No—I sing! I sing because I am a singer. If I use you in this way, it is because I have need of your ears!
>
> —Max Stirner, *The Ego and His Own*, translated by Steven T. Byington.

Postcard featuring Max Stirner's birthplace by Kunstverlagsanstalt Bruno Hansmann, Cassel. (no date)

Max Stirner Bibliography—Supplement Three 91
Trevor Blake (2019)
Max Stirner Bibliography (OVO: Portland, 2016) by Trevor Blake is the most complete bibliography of Max Stirner ever published in English. Happily, more commentary on Stirner has emerged and will likely emerge for decades to come. *Der Geist* will publish addendum to *Max Stirner Bibliography* until these additions are gathered in a future edition.

An Introduction to *Der Eyntsiger un Zayn Eygentum* 95
Trevor Blake, Kevin I. Slaughter (2019)

Der Eyntsiger un Zayn Eygentum 97
Y. A. Merison (Yiddish Original) (1916)
Union of Egoists, English trans. (2019)

Max Stirner Bibliography Addendum for 2019
Trevor Blake (2019)

Brockhaus' Kleines Konversations-Lexikon
(Leipzig: F. A. Brockhaus 1911) page 644:

Schmidt, Kaspar, Philosoph.

∉

"Man Versus the Superman" by Rev. J. Neville Figgis.
Welsh Outlook Volume 1 Number 10 (October 1914) page 420:

Germany or rather Prussia, if she attains world-empire, would in the same way propagate her own ideas and with them perhaps a new world-religion. This religion would be some development of Nietzsche's gospel of *The Will to Power*, the title of one of his later and most illuminating works. That is what we mean by saying that Nietzsche is the torch that lit this flame. Not that Nietzsche's doctrine was altogether new. Many of his most characteristic ideas came to him from an earlier and little-known writer, Max Stirner. Much more is little beyond an idealisation of Napoleonism.

∉

"Sacco and Vanzetti as I Knew Them" by Leonard D. Abbott.
Freedom Volume XLI Number 445 (September-October 1927) page 43:

It is untrue to say that Sacco and Vanzetti were not genuine Anarchists. They had minds capable of weighing and understanding the fine points of Anarchist theory, and they had the enthusiasm which made them want to devote their lives to the spreading of Anarchist ideas. They seemed, both, to be in a special sense admirers of Proudhon, but Vanzetti had studied closely the writings of Peter Kropotkin and Elisee Reclus, and Sacco was reading Max Stirner's *Ego and His Own* at the time when I talked with him.

¢

Masthead to *Freedom* Volume 11 Number 44 (November 12th, 1938):

The State rests on the slavery of labour. If labour becomes free, the state is lost. —Max Steiner [sic] (*The Ego and His Own*).

¢

Masthead to *Freedom* Volume 20 Number 9 (February 28th, 1959):

"What good is it to sheep that no-one restricts their freedom of speech? They never do anything but bleat." —Max Stirner, *The Unique One*.

¢

Stirnerism by R. L. in *Freedom* Volume 26 Number 29 (September 18th, 1965) page [2]:

The Ego and His Own. Max Stirner. 15s. A more revolutionary work than this has yet to be written. The case for the individual against authority is dealt with most profoundly. Most people who read it with care and have patience will discover that they have been slavish to an idea: to an idea of god, of country, of a nation, of humanity, mankind and so many causes which are in fact abstractions; 'wheels in the head' as the author would say. In the light of Stirner's work one observes that democracy is sham liberty, egoism the real liberty. What is free speech to sheep? They only bleat. Those who accept Stirner's teaching will take their liberty; they will bow the knee to no man, to no god, to no king, queen, nor belted earl, not even to any truth. Truths cannot move nor develop like a you or an I. Truths can be chains forged by one's own mind. Free thought means thoughts are free. Thoughts above me are free and can be my dominion. But my thoughts, my own thought, I am master of. In thinking slavish thoughts I as creator become the creature; a slavish creature of my own creation. In annihilating slavish thoughts I remain my own.

∉

"The Island" by Roger Jones. From *Science Fantasy*, edited by Kyril Bonfiglioli. Volume 23 Number 69 (January and February 1965) page 65:

"I do not surrender to you, I only wait." (Stirner)

∉

Incunabula Press Catalog 1990 / 1991 by Emory Cranston:[1]

Stirner, Nietzche & Stone Age Economy - an Examination of Non-authoritarian Hunter / Gatherer Societies.

∉

"Frederick Engels / Life of a Revolutionary" by Lindsey German. *International Socialism Journal* Issue 65 (Winter 1994):

Marx and Engels' first written collaboration in 1844 was *The Holy Family*, or as they originally called it, *A Critique of Critical Criticism* (the final title was regarded as more punchy but worried Engels who thought it would offend his religious father). In 1846 they wrote *The German Ideology*, subtitled *Critique of*

---

[1]   *Incunabula Press Catalog 1990 / 1991* by Emory Cranston was found by Joseph Matheny circa 1990. This catalog is part of the mystery of Ong's Hat. On pages four and five of the *Catalog* is a listing for a xerox of a mimeographed flyer titled "Course Catalogue for 1978-79, Institute of Chaos Studies and Imaginal Yoga." The listing here is found in the "Course Catalog."

modern German philosophy according to its representatives Feuerbach, Bruno Bauer and Stirner. Its aim was to attack the ideas which dominated German philosophical and political thinking. These the two regarded as mystical and idealist, because they started from ideas in the abstract rather than a materialist analysis. The weight of Marx and Engels' argument was that an understanding of the world had to start, not from the ideas which existed in people's heads in any particular historical period, but from the real, material conditions in which these ideas arose. Their starting point was therefore an understanding of the historical development of class society and how people's ideas altered in this process of social change.

"There Was No Sound of Thunder" by David Erik Nelson.
From *Asimov's Science Fiction,* edited by Sheila Williams.
Volume 38 Number 6 (June 2014) page 52:

[He] was the most seriously justice-minded guy I'd ever met. He'd actually read Stirner and Bakunin and Kropotkin and Goldman, and understood them, and had opinions about them that actually *meant* something. Also, he was basically the first guy I'd met since middle school who didn't ogle me and then try to impress my pants off - or at least my bra.

An Introduction to *Der Eyntsiger un Zayn Eygentum*
Trevor Blake, Kevin I. Slaughter (2019)

Max Stirner (1806-1856) was the author of *Der Einzige und sein Eigentum*, the fountainhead of egoism. The work was published in 1907 by Benjamin R. Tucker as *The Ego and His Own* in an English translation by Stephen T. Byington. It was published by Kropotkin Literatur Gezelshaft of New York in 1916 as *Der Eyntsiger un Zayn Eygentum* in a Yiddish translation by Y. A. Merison, also known as Jacob Abraham Maryson (1866-1941). This issue of *Der Geist* publishes the foreword matter of the Yiddish edition of Stirner newly translated into English for the first time. This Yiddish to English translation was commissioned by the Union of Egoists in 2019, and we thank Hershl Hartman for his exceptional work. Mr. Hartman makes the following comments on his translation:

> 1. The text uses the term *zakh*, which can mean "thing" or "cause." I have relied on context to determine which meaning to use.

> 2. Merison's introduction is in good Yiddish. His translation, however, relies heavily on the original German to the extent that, for example, a key word—reason—is rendered in a German word that was never incorporated into Yiddish and required research in an online German-English dictionary. Many other German-origin words and terms existed only in archaic Yiddish and were to be found in almost-ancient Yiddish-English dictionaries.

> 3. As there were no italics in Yiddish type fonts until relatively recently, the practice was to s p a c e o u t words that authors wished to emphasize. I have chosen to use italics, instead.

> 4. Too, Yiddish lacking capital letters, I have used my judgment in capitalizing concepts (Truth, Justice, etc.) and have followed standard usage in capitalizing God, He, Him, His,

etc. In both cases, my motive was to make the text more understandable to the English reader.

5. Brackets [ ] enclose my clarification comments. Parentheses ( ) appear as in the text.

Merison was an early editor of *Fraye Arbeter Shtime* (English: The Free Voice of Labor), the longest-running anarchist periodical in the Yiddish language.[1] He was fired after refusing to publish an article which praised the Communist Party of Russia. Merison also translated Charles Darwin, Herbert Spencer, Henry David Thoreau and others.

---

1 *Immigrants against the State: Yiddish and Italian Anarchism in America* by Kenyon Zimmer

DER EYNTSIGER UN ZAYN EYGENTUM
Y. A. MERISON (YIDDISH ORIGINAL) (1916)
UNION OF EGOISTS, ENGLISH TRANS. (2019)

Introduction

This book,"The Individual and His Property," that lies here before the reader, is a remarkable work in more than one sense. First, it has a remarkable history. In 1844 a book appears by an almost-unknown author which evokes a major tumult among the most radical thinkers of its time. Everyone talks about it; everyone feels to be under attack by it; everyone takes to criticizing it: no one, however, gets to its foundation, no one beats back its sharp analysis, and soon all fall silent and the book is forgotten. For fifty years, more or less, the book wanders about just so in the dust of libraries and no one, other than an individual thinker or a history writer, even mentions its name. Suddenly, an interest in the book is awakened. Reklam's publishing house issues a cheap version and it is sold by the thousands. Translations of the book appear in almost all European languages. There appear some large and sympathetic reviews of the book by well-known scholars, in addition to quite a few articles in the periodic press. In short,"The Individual and His Property" has been resurrected.

The second remarkable aspect and uniqueness of the book consists actually of its content itself. Its thesis is the elucidation and substantiation of egoism; but no matter how ingeniously this idea is defended in the work, it is no more remarkable than the defense of many other correct but one-sided principles. The main remarkableness is its *unheard-of heresy*. For thousands of years people have been enslaved to gods, beliefs, faiths which ruled over humans' lives, over their behaviors. By effort and exertion, in the course of generations, all sorts of heretical thoughts broke through one after another fortress of the gods until the radical idea "rediscovered the human being and raised him to the highest rank." The greatest achievement of heretical progress was that it abolished the importance of the relationship "between man and God" and raised to the highest the relationships of "man to man." Humanity, society and its morality, the people and its interests, the concepts of right and justice, freedom, equality, love of humanity—these strong towers were built on the ruins of gods and faiths. Radical thought often dared to purify the chaff of "man to man," to criticize societal institutions, breathe air into out-of-date morality, to basically democratize the life of the people—but to place a hand on the foundation of these humanly-holy relationships, to abolish the sacredness of the "man to man" ideals themselves. No one had ever dared to do this as did Stirner!

"Who cares about good, who cares about bad!" Stirner cries. "I am not good, not bad. Neither one makes any sense to me. Truth, freedom, humanity, justice, etc. want that I should serve them. An end to them! For me, there is nothing over me!"—Where and when in the history of human literature, before him or after him, did anyone dare to express such extremely heretical ideas? The most radical thought of the old world was reached at one side by the hedonism of Epicurus, and on the other side by the pessimistic "all is vanity" of Ecclesiastes. The only great heretic after Stirner—Friedrich Nietzsche, who with his daring re-evaluation of all values recalled the world of Stirner and contributed to its resuscitation—seeks to drive off the earth the morality of the weak and the weak themselves, in order that their place be taken by the strong, the super-human and the morality of strength. And he raises a new ideal for us—the ideal of self-abnegation in order to make room for this super-human, the true "chosen ones." Stirner is the only one who does not bow his head either to the past or to the future; who denies every morality and disparages every ideal; who does not even idealize the true egoist, because "every person does what he can and cannot be different than he is."

"The Individual and His Property" is also considered a classic of Anarchism in that it destroys through its sharp criticism the force of State and Law and generally every form of rule over the individual. However, the anarchist who will delight in devouring the pearls of wisdom by this deep-thinking critic will soon choke on the fulminations that the greatest heretic of all times pours out upon every ideal, not excluding Anarchism. "*People* means the body, *State* means the spirit of that *Ruling Person* who has oppressed me eternally,"—says Stirner. And he continues: "They say that you should be a whole, free person. But with this they proclaim a new *religion*, a new absolute, an ideal of freedom. Because religion consists of the dissatisfaction of the subjective person, i.e., in the creation of a '*peoples' commonality*' toward which one must strive, in the creation of an *ideal*." And so there can develop *missionaries* of freedom, just as Christianity created missionaries of faith; freedom can only be established, like the church, as a new community from which will emerge the same 'propaganda.'

Stirner does not omit any societal concept upon which he doesn't direct his sharp knife of critique: State, Right, Duty, Law, Freedom, Property, etc., are disassembled and disclosed in their nakedness and absence of content. His analysis cuts like a Roentgen-beam [x-ray] through the thick covering of these concepts and reveals a silhouette of superstition that lies at the base of our convictions about their worth and necessity. He distills their quintessence—godliness, Christianness, holiness—and resolves it: he "isolates the 'bread of affliction' and gets rid of it"…he finds that "the State has the purpose of *Christianizing* the people." "Everything that relates to the principle of morality belongs to the State." "He erects *holy* duties." "The Law is *holy*." "Punishment makes sense only as an atonement for the violation of something *holy*." "Freedom is a *Christian* concept." "Property in the civil sense denotes *holy* property."

The author also places under his knife the three revolutionary movements of his time, political, social and humanistic liberalism, and demonstrates how the holy spirit, the devil, the phantom has remained ingrained in them to force and enslave the individual. Political liberalism abolished inequality between the lords and their servants, it made people *lordless*: the lord, however, was changed into the phantom-law or State. Social liberalism had abolished the inequality of ownership, of rich and poor: property, however, was withdrawn from the individual and given into the hands of the phantom society. Humanitarian liberalism makes people godless, atheistic; but instead of the God of the individual, the God of everyone is upraised, *the person* in abstraction. Nothing has been fundamentally changed: "As the lord is reborn as the State, the servant again appears as the governmental subject; as ownership is transferred to societal property, concern is reborn as labor; and as God becomes condemned as a person, there arises a new faith—belief in the person or in freedom."

The heretic usually tends to overreach, to exaggerate on the other side, to over-salt and over-pepper; and so we find in this book much that shocks us, that causes us to shiver due to the paradoxical form of expression and primitive fearlessness of treatment. "The decline of nations and humanity will invite *me* to the emergence." "What do I care for the welfare of the community?" "Anything that is sacred is a binding, a chain." "What I can take by force I take by force, and what I cannot take by force is something to which I have no right." "I do not want freedom, I don't want equality of people; I want only *my* power over them because they create property for me. And if it doesn't work out for me, then…I do not even reject my power over life and death."

In essence, though, these angry heretics are also quite nice people, no worse than those so-called "good ones." Even the extreme egoist who screams that he doesn't care about the welfare of the community also cannot crawl out of his own skin; and his skin encloses an old, old, heritage of altruistic feelings that often cause him to sacrifice for the welfare of the community. Stirner, who is contemptuous of the whole world and cries out: "The people is dead, I shall live!" would nevertheless have given his life so that people would listen to his contempt…He says: "I can risk for another my life, my welfare, my freedom. This comprises my satisfaction and my joy, to delight in his joy and his satisfaction." And further: "I also love the people—not only individuals, but everyone. But I love them with the consciousness of egoism; I love them because love makes *me* joyful; I love, because it natural for me to love, because it pleases me."

Much differently, basically, the altruist does not say. He also asserts no more than that it is *natural* for a person to love another, that a person enjoys the other's joy and pleasure and that makes him joyful himself. The difference is found only in placing the emphasis: the egoist says "I love them because love makes *me* joyful;" the altruist says, "I love them because *love* makes me joyful." Stirner senses at once in the italicized word "love" a sacredness, an ideal, resulting in a *commandment*, so he therefore underlines the '*me*.'" The scientific position—upon which Kropotkin, for instance, bases Anarchistic morality—dispenses completely with the conscious "give us what is ours"-declaration and does not emphasize either love nor *me* but declares: "I love them because I can do nothing else, because it is natural for me to love due to an unconscious impulse that is rooted in my inborn social instinct."

In his zeal to smash all nets and uproot all sacredness, Stirner underestimates the importance of the enshrined ideals for human progress. Human progress in and for itself may not, as an egoist, concern him; but we must not forget that my progress as an individual depends very much on general progress. Self-assertion is certainly the axis upon which the wheel of progress revolves, but self-interests are not the only strengths that rotate the wheel; the motifs of love, of rights and justice play a large role in the movement of societal life. If it is accepted that power entitles one to everything and "what I cannot take by force is something to which I have no right," one tears out by the roots the main motif of every uprising to establish improvement—the motif of the raped feeling of justice. If right is truly no more than might, my heart cannot be aroused over any forceful act of the mighty and all that I can do is to place my strength against his. Stirner correctly understands the logic of the situation and does not fear to state: "Thereby war is declared by everyone against everyone."

The purpose of the egoist is, however, not constant war but the *balance* that must arise from it. Stirner finds this balance in the "Society of Egoists," to which everyone volunteers a part of his freedom in order to enjoy the uses of unification. He makes the quite correct comment that just as the wealthy are guilty for the fact that there are the poor, so the poor are guilty for the fact that there are the wealthy; and lets us draw the conclusion that the weak can unite against the strong and—we would say: *demand their rights*; Stirner says: *exert their power*. He is also sufficiently revolutionary to remark that "the poor become free and become owners only when they make an uprising, rise up and raise up themselves." But he does pose an ideal of a future society. He says: "They will ask, what will be then when the non-owners will gain courage? What sort of equalization will then take place?—You could just as well ask of me to foretell the fate of a newborn child. What a slave may do after having smashed his chains, that must be—anticipated."

Stirner's great accomplishment consists mainly in helping people smash so many chains. And even when we cannot agree with him that *every* holiness is a chain; when even the heavy hammer with which he so powerfully strikes at our chains sometimes tears off a piece of living flesh—when even his courageous contempt of all our ideals and holinesses grates so sharply in our ears—we must yet consider "The Individual and His Property" as one of the most inspiring educational works of all of world literature, and the author—one of the great contributors to humanity.

Dr. Y. A. Merison

In translating this book I sought as far as possible not to change the author's original style and I hope that I have succeeded in transmitting in Yiddish most of the word-play that he uses so often in the text.

In some portions in which the author polemicizes with representatives of other movements and provides his condemnations of their arguments, I have allowed myself to separate their words from his oppositional opinions in the form of a dialogue. These small changes help, in my opinion, to more clearly evince the sense of the debate and avoid a probing masculinity [seeking] to carry on over literal meanings. At other places, where there was required an explanation of an added word, I enclosed such words in brackets [ ] to indicate that they are not the author's.

Y. A. M.

FREE SPIRITS

The Eagle and The Serpent (1898–1927) was for a time published with the subtitle "A Journal of Free Spirits and for Spirits struggling to be Free." *The Eagle and The Serpent* favorably quotes Joseph A. Labadie in issue 18 (circa 1902), and later, in 1936, his son Laurance Labadie would use "A Journal for Free Spirits" as the subtitle for his own journal, *Discussion*. Laurance in turn was an influence on Mark A. Sullivan, who chose the same subtitle for his own gay individualist anarchist publication *The Storm* in 1976. In this same spirit, in this section, *Der Geist* collects "free spirits" too individualistic for other sections of our journal.

E.H. Fulton, publisher of *The Egoist* and other journals, and his daughter, at their home in Clinton, Iowa, 1925. Care of Labadie Photograph Collection, University of Michigan.

A History of the Radical Book Shop of Chicago **105**
Kevin I. Slaughter (2019)
A major piece of original research completed for *Der Geist*, the first history of a small, but influential anarchist/wobbly bookstore.

An American Anarchist **131**
Lilian Hiller Udell (1914)
From *The Little Review* Volume 1 Number 7 (October, 1914) pages 42-44. Voltairine de Cleyre (1866 – 1912) was an individualist anarchist.

Revolutionary Essays **134**
Lillian Hiller Udell (1914)
This review first appeared in *The International Socialist Review* Volume 15 Number 1 (July, 1914). That issue featured the short story "South of the Slot" by Jack London.

Three Tributes to Georgia Replogle **138**
(various) (1904)
Georgia Replogle and Henry Replogle were co-editors of the journal *Egoism* (1890). Georgia struggled with her health for many years, and died in 1904. These three tributes appear in *Lucifer the Light-bearer* No. 1026 (November 10th, 1904). The "biographical sketch" promised was printed in *Liberty* Volume 14, Number 24, (December 1904). J. Wm Lloyd's touching memorial article was reprinted in *Egoism: The First Two Volumes* (Underworld Amusement: Baltimore 2017).

Three You Cannot Afford to Do Without **140**
Trevor Blake (2019)
Three identical advertisements for *The Eagle and The Serpent* from three different periodicals.

Humanity First Letterhead **142**
John Basil Barnhill (circa 1919)

The Man Born Blind **143**
Ambrose Bierce (1888)
Aside from a map of the Black Hills region, Ambrose Bierce (1842 – 1914) had yet to publish a book under his own name when the following poem appeared in Benjamin R. Tucker's *Liberty* Volume 5 Number 25, whole number 129 (July 21st, 1888).

Joel's Literary Corner **145**
Carlo de Fornaro (1911)

Poems from the Imp **147**
Benjamin DeCasseres (1916-1921)

The Altruists' Corner **154**
Trevor Blake & Kevin I. Slaughter (2019)

A History of the Radical Book Shop of Chicago
Kevin I. Slaughter (2019)

> "I believe in the human intellect. I believe in demonstrating the value of my own individual type. I believe in demonstrating the value of Me to the universe. I am in search of freedom and now, at least, I am free."—Lillian Udell, 1915

The Radical Book Shop was founded in 1914 by disillusioned social worker Howard "Harry" Lewis Udell (1870-1918) and his blind wife Lillian Evangeline (Hiller) Udell (1867-1935), a respected lecturer on literature. Their daughters, Geraldine (1903-1998) and Phyllis (1900-1973), would assist and became integral to the running of the shop.

The "shoebox-sized" Radical Book Shop was a source for anarchist, unionist, socialist and communist material for decades. It was a place where radicals of all kinds would find inspiration and camaraderie. It became home to poets, revolutionaries, novelists, roughnecks, amateur actors, and attempted murderers of the heads of church and state. It was the only shop brave enough to openly sell Ragnar Redbeard's *Might is Right* before the Dil Pickle Club reprinted it.

While Howard died a few years in, Lillian became known as the "godmother of Chicago's hobohemia."

The egotheist Malfew Seklew was a frequenter, and it was there that Jack Jones began his weekly meetings that grew into the legendary Dil Pickle Club. Founder of the Industrial Workers of the World William "Bill" Haywood was often found there holding court by the wood stove, and "Father of the Beats" Kenneth Rexroth could be seen kissing the owners' daughter on the stage in the back, one that was part of the burgeoning Little Theater movement. "Anarchist balls" were held annually to fund raise for the shop. Later it became part of a co-op founded by Sherwood Anderson and compatriots, though, eventually, it was dropped from the scheme for terminal unprofitability.

It is unclear when the Radical Book Shop finally closed its doors (but it carried on into the late '20s at least). This humble little family-run shop sent ripples through the culture that can still be felt today, however faint. While there are mentions of the store in a number

Cover of *What is to be done? Life* by *Lyof N. Tolsoi* (Thomas Y. Crowell Co., New York, 1899) (reduced) with overset book trade label from the Radical Book Shop (enlarged), scanned from the title page.

of popular biographies and newspaper accounts through the years, it seems there was not one singular history. I have attempted to put together a history of the shop as it has had an impact not just on the culture of radical politics but on that of American avant-garde poetry and theater as well.. It does not end in a bang, but there are at least a few on the way.

DISAFFECTED UNITARIANS

Howard L. Udell was born in St. Louis on June 28th, 1870. He was ordained a Unitarian minister in 1896 and ministered to churches in Illinois, Wisconsin, and Michigan for the next 8 years. From 1905, he ran Associated Charities in a number of states, including Connecticut, Rhode Island, and Chicago. In 1908, he organized the Society for the Relief of Tuberculosis for the Associated Charities in Pawtucket.[1] In Connecticut in 1911, he advocated for juvenile courts and probation work so that "delinquent" children would not be stigmatized as criminals but instead be helped by probation officers and their families to correct the course of their lives.[2] In 1912, H.L. Udell took part in the 14th Annual Meeting of the American Hospital Association in Detroit, Michigan. On January 1st, 1914, Harry officially resigned from his position as Secretary of Associated Charities in Detroit.

Udell was described as "absolutely broken in health" by assistant secretary Mary Hubert:

> Mr. Udell will never admit his health is broken, but those who have watched him for the last three months know that the long hours, the tremendous number of investigations and reports which have come under his supervision, have told upon his health and have made it necessary for him to resign.[3]

Another source tells a different story, though, one in which Howard was so frustrated with how poorly social services and other organizations helped the poor and working classes, he quit in disgust to

---

1   *The Survey: Social, Charitable, Civic: A Journal of Constructive Philanthropy.* December 18, 1909.
2   "Probation" *The Survey*, March 18, 1911.
3   "H.L.Udell Quits; Broken in Health" Detroit *Free Press*, Nov. 18, 1913.

explore more radical ideas.

Lillian, born in Dunkirk, N.Y., was a women's rights activist and lecturer in literature. There are notices of her speaking on "Feminism in Literature",[1] Irish Poetry, and Ibsen. The Freeport Illinois *Daily Journal* on Feb. 8, 1897, in reporting a forthcoming lecture of hers on "Our Literary Idols" at the Globe Hall, quotes the *Kalamazoo News*:

> Mrs. Udell brings that rare combination of sympathy and critical judgement which enables one to get the best from such an author without blindly worshipping his faults and eccentricities.
>
> Her fine and accurate knowledge of general literature and familiarity with marked phrases of thoughts, past and present, were made apparent in the course of an address that was classic in every sentence, though delivered very simply with no attempt at oratorical effect. Mrs. Udell is a scholar and a thinker who deserves and will win the appreciation of those who care for both common and uncommon sense in dealing with the great questions and great writers of the day.
>
> The unusual culture of her mind is the more remarkable that it has been gained under the profound disability of total blindness since the second year of her age. In presence she is graceful and gracious, and voice, language and thought all betoken extreme refinement and sensitiveness of soul.

Lillian was blind since her childhood, though some stories (most certainly wrong) claim it happened later in life. In 1889, "Mrs. H.L. Udell" of Michigan was listed as being indebted to, among many other women, the American Women Suffrage Association for "State reports." In 1891, "Mrs. H.L. Udell" was listed as a "local committee" in the souvenir book for the 19th Congress of the Association for the Advancement of Women that took place in Grand Rapids, MI. She attended the Meadville Theological Seminary[2] but left without graduating in 1893.

Lillian was one of the handful of people who formed the Junior Humane Society at the McLaren School on April 18th, as reported in

---

1   "Announcements" *The Day Book*, July 10th, 1916.

2   *The Unitarian: A Monthly Magazine of Liberal Christianity*, Vol. IX, No. 12, December 1894.

the Vol. 8 No. 7, May 1913 issue of *Humane Advocate*, a publication of the Illinois Humane Society.

It's unclear when Harry and Lillian were married, but there is an essay in Benjamin R. Tucker's journal *Liberty* on the topic of Ibsen from Vol. 11, No. 4 (whole no. 316), June 29, 1895, that was signed "Mrs. Howard Udell".

In the Vol. XV, No. 1, July 1914 issue of the *International Socialist Review*, under the name "Lillian Hiller Udell" we find an essay titled "Revolutionary Essays" (reprinted in this issue). It puts to question "Has Socialism a literature?" and sets about answering that.

FROM SIDEWALK TO SHOEBOX, A STORE IS BORN

The bookstore was a hub for radical literature[1], sold tickets to Emma Goldman lectures, and even became part of the burgeoning "little theater" movement. Beginning at 954 N. Clark Street, it was just around the corner from the Oak Hall that served as a meeting place for "Wobblies" and where they would hold fundraising dances in the early days. There was great overlap between the frequenters of Radical Book Shop and the Dill Pickle Club[2]. Through Howard Udell's membership, the store had close ties to the Industrial Workers of the World, founded in Chicago in 1905. The "Wobblies" were social revolutionaries, advocating the replacement of capitalism with "industrial democracy" and doing so through organizing workers and going on strike.

One of the habitués of the Radical Book Shop was egoist author Malfew Seklew, who is said to have gone there to read the dictionary to expand his already verbose vocabulary.

The June 1914 issue of Charles H. Kerr's *International Socialist*

---

1 One such journal was *The Messenger*, founded in 1917, in New York City, by Chandler Owen and A. Philip Randolph; it was a journal integral to the growth of the Harlem Renaissance.

2 The Dil Pickle Club was frequented by such notable figures as author Ben Hecht, artist Stanisław Szukalski (who had a studio next door), egotheist Sirfessor Wilkesbarre (*aka* Malfew Seklew), Carl Sandburg, and the "whorehouse doctor" Ben Reitman. Mae West, Clarence Darrow, Mary MacLane, Magnus Hirschfeld, and Max Bodenheim all spoke or performed there. The Dil Pickle Club published the 1927 edition of *Might is Right* by Ragnar Redbeard, the last edition published in the author's lifetime. Franklin Rosemont's book *The Rise & Fall of the Dil Pickle Club* (Chicago, Charles H. Kerr) is highly recommended.

Title pages to three books ink-stamped by the Radical Book Shop
to mark its passage through their store.

Review contained the following notice:

> **A Radical Book Shop.**—For a long time a perception has been growing among thinking people that Chicago needed headquarters for all radical literature. Such a shop has been opened at 954 North Clark street. Send in your orders for any book you want and when in the city don't fail to call. Lowest prices on all books pertaining to free thought in religion, science, economics, feminism and all departments of sociology. Address all correspondence to Radical Book Shop, 954 North Clark street, Chicago.

And while the *International Socialist Review* gives its story of the creation of this interesting little place that has had a lasting impact on the arts and politics, an April 2nd, 1916 article in the *Chicago Tribune* tells a different, less idealistic story. As part of Fanny Butcher's "Tabloid Book Review" column in the Sunday edition, she said,

> A couple of years ago (Howard and Lillian Udell) were actually in want. To keep from starving they took the books from their unusual library, spread them out on some boards across an alley in North Clark street, and for two days they held their little street shop. Passersby stopped at the unusual sight, and stopped longer when they read the titles of the books for sale.
>
> Then a man came along, a man who owned a cubby hole of a shop near the alley. "You can't have a shop here," he said, meaning the alley, "but you can here," meaning the cubby hole. They moved into the little twelve foot place. Mr. Udell put up book shelves. Friends of his I.W.W. workers, eager young anarchists every one, turned in and helped. Books that couldn't be found in the élite book shops were to be had there.

Around this time, the Radical Book Shop was placing half and full page ads in Chicago's arts journal *The Little Review*, edited by Margaret C. Anderson.[1] That journal was the American "sister" of Dora Mars-

---

1   *The Little Review* was a staple journal at the Radical Book Shop, along with *The Arts*, *Others* and many of the literary journals.

den's journal *The Egoist*,[1] a journal Marsden founded and wrote for.

The first and best description of their second location comes from a love story serialized in the *Chicago Tribune* in 1915. The series was titled "The Love Letters of a Lonely Girl," and finding a passing reference to the bookshop is delightfully incongruous for a story that begins "Big Dear you: Here is Little Me for a talk with you again." From the third installment (April 4th), I excerpt the pertinent section:

> En route homeward my eye caught a curious sign—an unpretentious board with "Radical Book Shop," in small letters, and beneath, in large letters, "Laundry," upon it. I stopped before the tiny window. Through it, beyond the books displayed, of Marx, Nietzsche, Tolstoi, and Breiux, I saw a tall pallid man reading to a woman. Her back was to the window. Curiosity impelled me in. What were they reading?
>
> "That's fine, dear," I heard her say as I closed the door on entering. Not more than two people could stand side by side within the shop, it was so small. There were perhaps half a hundred books on the shelves; they were fierce, bristley looking sort of books—I didn't recognize them, even by name, except Tolstoi and Brieux. Half ashamed of my curiosity—for this place did not seem a shop to prowl about in, somehow—I stammered out that I wanted "The House of Pomegranates." The woman arose and came forward gropingly. Then I saw—she was blind! No, they did not have it; they carried only radical books.
>
> I was humbled and awed before her. The little shop had suddenly become a sanctuary.

There was a sizable write-up on the bookstore in the *Chicago Tribune* of May 11th, 1915 noting that half the "tiny box of a room" was the book shop, the other half was a "3 cent lunch," and the sign out front advertised their hand laundry services. The article listed the types of reformers and revolutionaries that would gather around the stove

---

[1] Ezra Pound was a one time literary editor of *The Egoist*, a foreign correspondent for *Poetry* magazine, and, in 1917, became foreign editor of *The Little Review*, though he still contributed articles to the prior. "In so far as it is possible, I should like *The Little Review* to aid and abet *The Egoist* in its work," Pound wrote in the Editorial of the May 1917 issue.

in the back of the shop: Socialists, single-taxers, philosophical anarchists, syndicalists, international New Thoughters, Industrial Workers of the World, bearers of the cosmic light, rationalists, Christian socialists and futurists. The lighthearted story gives an anecdote under the subheading "Anarchist No More":

> During the noon hour, while Mr. and Mrs. Udell were at luncheon, the shop was left in charge of their two small daughters. And it may surprise the parents to learn that their eldest, a pretty child of 14, has recently deserted her inherited belief in philosophical anarchy.
> "I used to be an anarchist," she said, "but I am not any longer. I changed just a few weeks ago. Somebody stole the rugs we put in our front hall, so that things would look a little nicer. And lots and lots of times somebody steals our bottles of milk. Of course I know the theory that they need the things more than we do. Perhaps they were hungry and did need the milk, but I don't see why they needed to take our rugs."

Another *Tribune* article from 1917 gave a further description: "The shop is about six feet wide and runs back twenty-eight or thirty feet. A bit of a two foot counter holds a cash register in front."

On October 25th, the Radical Book Store made it to the "Society and Entertainment" column when socialite Virgina Pope[1] stepped into the store:

> That society maids do interest themselves in other things than dancing, bridge, and tea parties was proven again last week when Miss Virginia Pope, daughter of Mrs. Francis Pope of 62 East Oak street, wandered into the Radical Bookshop (sic), that unique bit of radical space at 817 North Clark street... and inquired into the principles of the place where gather many interesting people for interesting discussion.
> So interested did she become in the attitude of ideas that she found there and in the two little girls, Phyllis and Geraldine,

---

[1] Virginia Pope moved to New York and joined the *New York Times* in 1925 where she would become fashion editor. A fashion designer named Pauline Trigere was quoted in Miss Pope's 1978 obituary: "I think she invented the reporting of fashion."

that she suggested afternoon teas where many of her fashionable friends would be eager to come and learn of the facts and fancies of the labor world.

Miss Pope has interested herself in equal suffrage for some time and is an active member of the association of that name, and no doubt will find much to be enthusiastic about in the activities that are discussed at the Radical Bookshop (sic), should her plan materialize.

THE ANARCHIST BALLS

The *Day Book*[1] newspaper of May 20th, 1915, mentioned the "friends of the Radical Book Shop" were organizing a dance to be held at Baker's hall (220 W. Oak St.) that Friday and tickets were 25 cents. This may have been the first of a series of similar events.

On April 6, 1916, the same paper featured an article titled "Expect a Big Time at the Radical Book Shop Ball."

> Socialists, single taxers, anarchists, I. W. W.'s, university settlement workers and birth controllers are all backing the Radical Book Shop ball Friday night in Oak Hall, 220 W. Oak st.
>
> Bill Haywood and Elizabeth Gurley Flynn will lead the grand march. Rev. Wm. Thurston Brown will give out programs. Henry M. Hyde, social justice editor of the *Tribune*, and Wm. L. Chenery, editor of The Guide Post in the *Herald*, will be there with bells on.
>
> "Every community ought to have a book store like the Radical Book Shop." said Edgar Lee Masters. "I like to step in there and see shelves of books sometimes called dangerous, but representing all shades of rebellion and protest. The shop is unique and its ball should be patronized. I don't agree with nine-tenths of its books, but I can see a healthy ferment from it."

---

1   *The Day Book* was an advertising free daily newspaper. It was available for sale at the Radical Book Shop, and Ralph Chaplin in his book *Wobbly: The Rough-And-Tumble Story Of An American Radical*, recalled Carl Sandburg picking it up there. Letters from the *Day Book* are featured in a significant part of the *Gospel According to Malfew Seklew* (Baltimore: Underworld Amusements) and the paper also ran the *The Outbursts of Everett True* comics compiled into a book (Baltimore: Underworld Amusements).

After some background information (already covered), it continues:

> Sometimes a real mixed crowd is caught in the hang-out. One afternoon, for instance, were standing around looking at books and talking, these:
> Jim Larkin, famous strike leader from Ireland; Edna Kenton, writer for the *Saturday Evening Post*, the *Bookman* and other magazines, also the author of one novel that was a "best seller"; two members of the I. W. W. national executive board from out of town; Fannie Butcher, special writer for the Tribune; Harry Herwitz, secretary to Ald. Merriam; three charity workers; Rev. J. C. Ashurst, a Baptist minister; Leslie H. Marrey, editor *International Socialist Review*; Margaret Merriman, actress with Chester Wallace Players, and stage people from the *So Long Letty*, *The Weavers* and the Little Theater companies.
> It is a sort of clearing house and news center for the radical world. The shop hasn't reached the point where It pays a living wage profit to the Udells. So its friends want to see a big crowd at the bail Friday night.

November 16th, 1916, saw a notice that a dance was being held at "Oak Hall" again, but no other notices have been found.

POISONING THE GOVERNOR, THE MAYOR AND THE ARCHBISHOP

On Feb 12th, 1916, a reporter found William D. "Bill" Heywood at the Radical Book Shop at 817 ½ N. Clark, surrounded by "a group of I.W.W. radicals." They were all reading newspaper accounts of an anarchist cook named Jean Crones, who tried to murder a couple hundred of Chicago's most powerful politicians, business men and even the Archbishop. George Mundelein became the third Archibishop of Chicago on December 9, 1915, and while initially it was thought that Crones was a German Agent, it was discovered he was an Italian anarchist named Nestor Dondoglio. Nestor was part of the Luigi Galleani circle of insurrectionary anarchists, known for their "propaganda of the deed." Galleani published a journal titled *Cronaca Sovversiva* (*Subversive Chronicle*) and it was said of him: "You heard Galleani speak,

Tribune

HOME EDITION

SIX PAGES. — THIS PAPER CONSISTS OF TWO SECTIONS—SECTION ONE. ★ PRICE TWO CENTS.

GOT 7 U-BOATS

CORONER SAYS

PATRIOTIC UTTERANCES

[Copyright: 1917: By John T. McCutcheon.]

U. S. SEIZES TWO TEUTON PAPERS AND 'RED' STORE

Arbeiter Zeitung and Demokratin Stripped.

Three raiding parties dashed away from the federal building last night and in a few minutes three more places had been seized under federal warrants in the government's campaign to suppress seditious and treasonable agitation. The places snagged by the department of justice are:

Chicago Arbeiter Zeitung, a German language labor-Socialist publication, 1642 North Halsted street, nicknamed "The Flaming Torch."

The Social Demokraten, a German language Socialist newspaper, 2003 North California avenue, said to have been very outspoken.

The Radical Book Store, 817½ North Clark street, where radical publications of many kinds are sold; long under surveillance.

BOLD IN CRITICISM.

These places were seized under warrants issued by Judge Evan Evans, identical with the eight he issued the day before the I. W. W. and other raids. The two German languages

Detail of the front page of the Chicago Tribune *(Chicago, Illinois) for Sep 7, 1917.*

and you were ready to shoot the first policeman you saw".[1]

Mark Jacob, in the *Chicago Tribune* noted:

> Illinois Gov. Edward Dunne was there, along with former Gov. Charles Deneen, former Chicago Mayor Carter Harrison Jr., utility czar Samuel Insull, bishops, bank presidents, judges and the superintendent of schools.

But while many got very sick, nobody actually died. There are slightly conflicting stories as to why this is. The one constant is that Dondoglio poured arsenic into the soup, but why it became diluted is up in the air. One source has it that due to an additional 50 guests being added to the party, the soup was diluted, while another says that another cook thought the broth had spoiled on taste-testing, and replaced most of it with new, unpoisoned stock.

"All I know is what I read in the newspapers", Heywood is reported to have said, in denial of knowing anything about the crime, or the man who perpetrated it. He denied that the man was a member of his organization. The I.W.W. members that were hanging out with "Bill" Heywood at the Radical Book Shop had a different theory: "It was a setup by the cops". Dondoglio was never caught, and died peacefully in Connecticut in 1932.

THE I.W.W. RAIDS

September 5th, 1917, saw the federal government raid IWW halls and offices across the country, arresting 165 members that would eventually see a Chicago trial where 100 of them were found guilty in court "of more than 10,000 individual violations of federal law." Theron P. Cooper was one of the leaders of the Industrial Workers of the World who were charged with conspiracy to obstruct the war in 1918. *Clarence Darrow: Attorney for the Damned* by John A. Farrell, a biography of the famed attorney, merely refers to Cooper as "a pacifist."

The next day more warrants were issued, but this time for two German-language newspapers and the Radical Book Shop. An article published in the *Chicago Tribune* the next day under the title "U.S. Seizes Two Teuton Papers and 'Red' Store" gave detail:

---

1 Avrich, Paul, *Anarchist Voices: An Oral History of Anarchism in America*, Princeton: Princeton University Press (1996)

Three raiding parties dashed away from the federal building last night and in a few minutes three more places had been seized under federal warrants in the government's campaign to suppress seditious and treasonable agitation. The places snagged by the department of justice are:

Chicago Arbeiter Zeitung, a German language labor-Socialist publication, 1642 North Halstead street, nicknamed "The Flaming Torch".

The Social Demokraten, a German language Socialist newspaper, 2003 North California avenue, said to have been very outspoken.[1]

The Radical Book Store, 817 1/2 North Clark street, where radical publications of many kinds are sold; long under surveillance.

BOLD IN CRITICISM.

These places were seized under warrants issued by Judge Evan Evans, identical with the eight he issued the day before the I.W.W. and other raids. The two German language newspapers, the federal officials say, have grown bold in their criticisms of the government.

The Radical Book store has been a sort of rendezvous for disgruntled individuals and the jobless who have come there to purchase radical books and pamphlets. There and in nearby saloons they have talked over their woes. The habitues of the immediate district have been "checked up" by the officials for two or three years back.

After some retelling of the raids on the newspapers the story focuses on the bookstore:

STORE STRIPPED.

When a reporter visited the Radical Book Shop a few minutes after the raid he found Harry L. Udell, its keeper, and his blind wife, in the dingy little shop where for years they

---

[1] Both of these papers were sold at the Radical Book Shop.

have earned a livelihood by selling radical and anarchistic literature. The shop is about six feet wide and runs back twenty-eight or thirty feet. A bit of a two foot counter holds a cash register in front. Udell and his wife declined to talk. But the walls of the obscure little place told the story mutely. An hour before socialistic and I.W.W. literature had lined the interior. Now there were blank places whence the "goods" had been torn.

The operatives evidently knew what they wanted: had the books and pamphlets they were to take spotted. They came in, worked swiftly, and were gone almost before the neighborhood knew they were there. No resistance was offered.

BITTER FOOD FOR THOUGHT.

Mrs. Udell, blind for years, had listened to the chatter of those who came to the shop for so long that she is known as a strong Socialist locally. She has visited around in the neighborhood and has spoken her mind freely. With the rest of the world shut out the little woman has sat in darkness and has had for a long time as her chief mental nourishment the embittered thoughts of agitators who knew the shop as their rendezvous.

The neighborhood used to be largely inhabited by Socialists who aired their views from curbs at night. Close by, at Chicago avenue and Clark street, above the saloon of "Spike" Hennessy, is a hall where the Socialist clan used to gather.

Down at Oak Street and Franklin is a Baker's Hall, also a rendezvous for a long time for Socialists and I.W.W. fanatics. In these places and in this neighborhood the police have been called many times and have dispersed many a rioting crowd.

ANTI-WAR CLANS BOOM TRADE.

Such was the neighborhood that used, in time gone by, to give the Radical Book Shop its bit of prosperity. Then for a long time it did not do so well. More recently anti-war agitators, pacifists, and pro-German propaganda spreaders have been active and business began to return.

In a way the sooty little book store, picturesque in itself, is said to be a sort of "official canteen" for the clans who gathered there after their own ways and to speak their own thoughts.

DEATH OF A FOUNDER AND A NEW LIFE

In 1918, "Harry" Udell died, leaving blind wife and two children destitute. The store never made money, and though Lillian was well known as a passionate, capable and intellectual woman, she was blind and had two girls to take care of.

The "Chicago Co-Operative Bookstores Company" was founded by novelist Sherwood Anderson[1] (who also frequented the Dil Pickle Club) I.W.W. activist and Harvard Alum. Theron P. Cooper issued shares for the store before moving it to 826 N. Clark St. Some stories falsely states that 1918 was the year the Radical Book Store was opened, but it was really a continuation "under new ownership."

A short piece written in 1919 by Guido Bruno[2] highlights the connection between the bookstore and the Dill Pickle Club[3]:

> The Radical Book Shop is right around the corner. It is a co-operative store with a large stock of ultra-radical pamphlets and magazines, the meeting place for all sorts of Bolsheviki, pleasant Bolsheviki, who want to intoxicate themselves with words rather than with deeds, who are more eager to have a good time under present conditions than to be martyrs for a new and better world. And when they want to amuse themselves, and be real radicals, they go around the block, to the Dillpickle. Mr. Johns, who is one of the co-operatives of the bookshop, is also one of the proprietors of the Dillpickle, a sort of restaurant, public forum, dance hall, and at present "the slum of Chicago," because some of its hangers-on were arrested as supposed bomb manufacturers during the recent I.W.W. trial.
>
> It is a sort of debating club, *a la* Greenwich Village, with automobiles in front of it after ten p.m. when the rich come to

---

1   According to *Sherwood Anderson's Secret Love Letters*, edited by Ray Lewis White (Louisiana State University Press, Baton Rouge, 1991) it was in 1920 the Radical Book Shop hosted one of two known exhibits of the paintings of Sherwood Anderson.
2   Published in *Adventures in American bookshops, antique stores and auction rooms* by Guido Bruno, (Detroit : The Douglas Book Shop, 1922).
3   There is no "correct" way to write the name of Jack Jones' club. Dil Pickle, Dill Pickle or Dillpickle as you see here are all more or less correct as seen on posters and promotional material from the club itself.

see the poor, the law-abiding want to have a peek at the lawless, the properly married to see the free-lovers.... Chicago is very young, you know! It is in its bootees. All these "new ideas" are here in flower of springtime. I once said, "Were there no Greenwich Village, one would have to be invented." Chicago invented its own. The Dillpickle will have many competitors soon, under the signs of flowers, vegetables and animals. In a couple of years they will become stale canned goods. And then the empty cans will be consigned to the ash can. Greenwich Village all over again!

A column titled "Frederic Haskin's Letter" from the *Rock Island Argus* newspaper of Sept. 14, 1920, detailing some Chicago bookstores, gives a bit of background of the new store. The article notes that it is run by a "gentle-voiced little lady, Mrs. Udell, assisted by her daughter Geraldine." It goes on "Its history is an interesting example of idealism, which however much we may disapprove of it, we cannot help but admire. In times of great emergency they sold one of the valued books from their private library, 'feeling like cannibals when we did so,' says Mrs. Udell."

BOOKS AND PAMPHLETS WHICH TELL THE truth. Send for catalogs. Radical Book Shop, Co-Operative, 867 North Clark St., Chicago, Ill.

Classified advertisement placed in *The Nonpartisan Leader*, February 07, 1921

The Walden Book Shop was opened by the co-op group as a second shop[1] at 311 Plymouth Court. Both stores were to be run on a cooperative basis. When a share holder bought a book at the shop, you would write your name and address on a form and at the end of the year a percentage of the profit of the purchase is returned to you. The *Rock Island Argus* column notes: "So far the percentage returned to purchasers has been so low as to be negligible, but... the shops are already paying dividends to the stockholders."

---

1 In January of 1927 an advertisement announced a "Removal Sale...before moving to 309 Plymouth Court". In June the address was still listed as 307 Plymouth Court in a trade publication, but by October of that year the address was listed as 311 Plymouth Court in an advertisement.

The April 16, 1921, issue of *The Publishers Weekly* printed the notice:

> CHICAGO.—The Radical Book Shop is moving to a new and larger store at 826 North Clark Street on May 1.[1]

A book on the history of the Co-operative Movement in Illinois[2] praised the Company founded by Anderson and Cooper. They detailed that 225 shares were sold at $5 a piece, but that there was a loss of $3,500 by 1922. A proposition to move the store to the "loop district" was opposed, and so stockholders of the Cooperative decided that because the Radical Book Shop ran at such a deficit, and only existed on profits of the Walden Book Shop, official ties should be severed. *The Publishers Weekly* for April 15th of 1922 carried the following notice:

> **Chicago, Ill.** - The Chicago Co-Operatives Book Store Company has sold out its interest in the Radical Book Shop located at 826 North Clark Street.

Mrs. Udell[3] took back management of the shop once more and Theron P. Cooper managed the Walden Book Shop.[4] It is unclear how long the Walden Book Shop was run as a co-operative.

The *Daily Worker* printed a celebratory notice on July 17th, 1924:[5]

---

1 The September 1922 issue of *The Publishers Weekly* still listed the address as 867, but in October it changed to 826.
2 *The Consumers Co-operative Movement in Illinois* by Colston Estey Warne, University of Chicago Press, 1926
3 A February 26, 1922 article in the *Chicago Evening American* gave Lillian's home address at the time as 168 W. Chicago Ave.
4 Co-operative opened a second store under the Walden name in 1924. A third was advertised as being opened in the Palmolive Building in 1929, and a fourth in the Michigan Square building at 546 North Michigan Avenue. The three story storefront of the latter is famous for its art-deco facade; the building it's in had a temple to Diana in the center, replete with pillars and a large statue of her by Swedish sculptor Carl Milles.
5 This author fails to see how an explicitly Communist paper could frame the more mainstream store being financially successful after casting off the more ideological Radical Book Store as "winning."

Walden Cooperative Bookshop Wins

The Chicago Cooperative Book Stores Company, has just completed a thorly (sic) successful year. This happens to be the first financially successful year of its short four year's existence. Organised in April, 1920, the Chicago Cooperative Book Stores Company opened two bookshops, the "Radical Book Shop" and the "Walden Book Shop." In 1922, the first of these was sold to another concern and all attention given to the making the Walden Book Shop a genuine co-operative success.

STUDIO PLAYERS

It was in July of 1922 that an announcement was made about the formation of the Studio Players in *The New Majority*[1] journal:

> Once in a while comes a period in which the commercial theaters let a few plays through that attack existing institutions or reflect on the present social or industrial order. For instance, at present the big theaters are running "Liliom," "Anna Christie." "The Hairy Ape." This must not lead us to believe that the theater is a free forum for expression.
>
> It is the little theater movement that blazes the trail in the effort to overcome the commercial censorship which (for varying reasons) keeps many plays off the stage. In Chicago a company has been formed called the Studio Players. Its home is in a little theater at the rear of the Radical Book Shop, 826 N. Clark street. Here, with all the intimate touch that is possible between players and audience in a room holding only fifty seats.
>
> Last week four performances were given of Ibsen's play, "The Lady From the Sea." Not by any means the best of Ibsen's plays, still it is a powerful protest against matrimonial enslavement and the use of the nuptial contract to deprive parties thereto of exercise of free will for life.
>
> The presentation was earnest, the play was so difficult as to try the abilities of the cast to the utmost. The best work was done by Phyllis Udell, who also had the most difficult role.

---

1   *The New Majority* was available for sale at the Radical Book Shop.

A positive review in *The New Majority* of September 2, 1922 detailed in somewhat of a compliment that the Studio Players gave a performance that was a "distinct advance over their work at the beginning of the summer season." The play this time was *The Importance of Being Earnest* by Oscar Wilde. "It was a snappy show, full of pep and fun," read the review in a manner that sounds if one was forced to satirize a review from the 1920s.

On March 28th 1923, the Poetry Club of the University of Chicago were reported to have held a meeting there where Jessica North, who was their president at the time, gave a reading.[1]

ROBOTS INVENTED FOR WEIRD COMMUNIST PLAY

In the most absurd revelations of the history of the Radical Book Club is in 1923, the Labor Defence Council staged a little theater performance of the science fiction play *R.U.R.* Written by the Czech writer Karel Čapek. "R.U.R." stands for Rossumovi Univerzální Roboti (Rossum's Universal Robots), a play that had premiered in a major theater in Chicago the year previously. Performed by the Studio Players, including, of course, Geraldine, and directed by the Players' Guy Woodson. It was Čapek's play that introduced the word Robot into the English language, deriving from a Czech word, *robota*, meaning "forced labor".

The Communist *Daily Worker's* hyperbolic announcement:

> The principal parts are being taken by actors and actresses of wide experience, who can be depended upon to put into the production all the force and fire and sarcasm and majesty that its Communist authors intended...
>
> The Labor Defense Council considers R.U.R. not only as a great drama but as an extraordinary piece of propaganda, one which cannot fail to burn its lesson deep into the mind of every proletarian. Thousands of workers are expected to witness the performances. The whole enterprise will be on a larger scale than anything of its kind ever attempted. All available resources will be mobilized to make it something which will be long remembered in the Chicago labor movement.

---

[1] North later succeeded Harriet Monroe as editor of *Poetry* magazine in 1936, after the latter's death, and co-edited the magazine with Peter De Vries from 1937 to 1942.

And then:

Six Robots Wanted.
To complete the cast, the Labor Defense Council is on the lookout for six sturdy Robots, to personify the product turned out in "Rossum's Universal Robot" factory. There is little or no speaking required of these "robots." A good robot—like a good wage slave—is one who does what he is told and says little. But in spite of the humbleness of their roles, the robots are as necessary to the cast of R.U.R. as the workers are to industry. The parts must be filled at once.

The notice ends:

> In the midst of the preparations for the staging of R.U.R, the Studio Players, who will be the back bone of the production, are continuing their own performances of out-of-the-ordinary plays in their little theatre back of the Radical Book Shop. Their next production will be Bernard Shaw's "Man and Superman."

All radical politics tend to create small circles (generally circular firing squads). Of note here is Lenetta M. Cooper, the wife of Theron Cooper, who worked at Plymouth St. branch of the Walden Book Store. Netta was one of the 21 persons on the National Committee of the Labor Defense Council that staged the play. The LDC was established by the Communist Party of America in September of 1922 as a fundraising group.

KENNETH REXROTH KISSES SISTER GERALDINE
In *An Autobiographical Novel* by Kenneth Rexroth, the poet details his meeting Sherwood Anderson in 1924. At the time he was borrowing books from the library on German Expressionism, Italian Futurism, the Symbolists. His dive into radical art was fueled by discovering the bookstore:

> About this time I discovered a source for the kind of books I wanted to read. The Radical Bookshop (sic) in the old North Side Turner Hall on North Clark Street started importing the

avant-garde poetry of the Twenties from France and Germany and Russia. In a short while they were also getting American and English books, published by the first Paris-Americans. I bought them all, and I only wish I had saved them, because they'd be worth a lot of money today. Nobody else wanted them, and I usually got them at considerable discount.

The Radical Bookshop (sic) had a Little Theater with a tiny stage in the back room. Here I acted in Shaw and Wedekind. For some reason I was usually cast as an old man, and while still in high school, heavily and amateurishly made up with Oxford glasses on a ribbon, I made a most flatulent Roebuck Ramsden. The Radical Bookshop (sic) was run by a frail, white-haired widow, Mrs. Udell, who was totally blind, and who was always accompanied by a blonde and a brunette daughter at her right and left hand, Geraldine and Phyllis. They had grown up in the Little Theater in the back room and knew by heart all the lines of all the desperate young misses in all the Theater of Revolt. I think they fancied themselves as considerably higher-brow Gish sisters, with a dash of Nazimova, and they were, rather. The mother was a Sibylline and sepulchral character straight out of a Greek oracle. She said almost nothing, and what she did say was ambiguous and intimidating. Phyllis was too nervous, too much on the Ida Rubinstein ride for me, but Geraldine was even calmer and more collected than her mother and not at all cryptic. All it ever came to was a kiss or two on the stage in a Wedekind tragedy of youngsters like ourselves.

It was possibly at the Radical Book Shop he picked up a copy of Wyndham Lewis' journal *The Blast*.

VINCENTE MINELLI STARTS AND QUITS ACTING
Husband of actress Lisa Minelli, Vincente recalls growing up in Chicago, and his brief stint in the theater of the Radical Book Shop, in his memoir *I Remember it Well:*[1]

I even made a half-hearted attempt at acting. A blind wom-

---

1   Minelli, Vincente. I *Remember it Well* (Doubleday & Company, Inc. Garden City, NewYork) 1974

an came in one day, accompanied by a young girl, asking to borrow some props from Mr. Frazier.[1] She was with a group which put on plays in a theater behind the Radical Book Shop on North Clark Street. They were doing an O'Neill one-acter. "Would you like to join our group?" the woman asked.

I reported to the theater to read for one of the lesser parts, and went into rehearsal the same night. It was one of O'Neill's greatest exercises in foreboding doom... a retired sea captain going mad, along with his son... given to many pregnant pauses, it seemed to me, and to frequent trips to the roof in order to symbolically find the meaning of life, a vision he would receive through his trusty telescope. I was going mad along with the captain and his son.

Next door was a dance hall separated from the theater by a plywood partition. We were blitzed by the yelling and cussing that accompanied the frequent free-for-alls on the other side of that thin wall. Sometimes, when some battler was knocked against the partition, it looked as if we would be brought into the action... I fully expected it to happen whenever that wall finally toppled.

One evening, an Irishman came into the theater. He'd just been released from jail after serving a sentence for some sort of organized anarchy. "We won't stop," he screamed, "until we hang every capitalist from the highest lamp post!" The troupe reacted to his ranting as if it were a commonplace occurrence, which it probably was, meeting his outburst with desultory cheers. That did it for me. I packed my gear and walked out, turning my back on acting forevermore. If the performing arts lost a bright light you can blame it on the Bolsheviks.

A JOB FOR GERALDINE, A FEW MORE PLAYS, THEN... NOTHING

Harriet Monroe, founder and then editor of *Poetry* magazine, hired Geraldine as her personal assistant in 1925, but "Gerry" continued acting in plays put on by the Studio Players, often directed by her sister Phyllis.

---

1   Mr. Frazier was the head of the display department of Marshall Field, a Chicago department store. Mr. Minelli got a job at as Mr. Frazier's fourth assistant in his late teens.

The *Daily Worker* printed this notice in 1925:

> Meeting of North Side workers will be held tonight at the Radical Book Shop. 826 N. Clark St., at 8 p.m.. under the auspices of the North Side Branch of the International Labor Defense.
>
> All readers of the DAILY WORKER residing in the North Side are welcomed at this gathering which will be of great interest, dealing as it will with the subject of the defense of class-war prisoners in America.
>
> Admission will be free. The speaker of the evening will be S. T. Hammersmark who will explain why the workers must organize for their defense on the political field.

The Daily Worker of Thursday October 12, 1926, had a notice that the Studio Players were performing *The Adding Machine* by Elmer Rice as a fundraiser for them at the Douglas Park Auditorium, but that they "give performances every Saturday and Sunday night at the Radical Book Shop, 826 North Clark street."

A February 6th, 1927 article in the Chicago Tribune noted that the Dill Pickle and Radical Book Shop were two of the oldest of the Bohemian scene in "Tower Town," a district around the Chicago Water Tower.

Later that year, in the same paper, it was announced that the play *The Cad*, written by Marion Strobel (known by "society" as Mrs. James Herbert Mitchell, her husband being a famous dermatologist), was well received by an audience of social radicals and social elites. It was performed by the Studio Players. Harriet Monroe was in attendance, and Geraldine Udell played the feminine lead in the production[1].

On September 19th, 1930, Lillian, Phyllis, and Geraldine arrived to the port of New York on the ship "Volendam" from Boulogne-sur-Mer, France. Lilian was 58, and the girls both in their late-20s and unmarried. They lived at 205 Ontario St. in Chicago at the time.

In November 14th, 1930, a newspaper account of the death of Theron P. Cooper was published. A six page letter was found where the author detailed his slow death as he was overtaken by gas left

---

[1] Marion Strobel was an "associate editor" of *Poetry* magazine for a short while. Geraldine Udell would step in as editor when Harriet was travelling in 1930s, and was officially the "Business Manager" of *Poetry* in April of 1947.

on in the kitchen. "I have heard that gas was an easy and quick way to die, but I have been writing now for 45 minutes and am still able to scribble." His brother Kenneth L. Cooper denied the accusation of suicide, saying he found his brother in the garage, overtaken by automobile exhaust fumes.

An announcement of September 24th, 1932, detailed a bankruptcy auction of Walden Book Shops[1] to be held at 546 N. Michigan Ave.[2]

In 1933 the Dil Pickle Club was shut down using an ordinance prohibiting dance-halls from being within 100 feet of a church.[3]

LILLIAN DIES, AND LIFE MOVES ON

The Radical Book Shop made no more news, at least none available to me. Lillian died in 1935 at her house at 523 Belden Ave. The obituaries that ran in the *Chicago Tribune* and *New York Times* were similar. The former called her the "'godmother' of most of Chicago's 'hobohemia,'" whereas the New York Times referred to her as the "mother of Chicago's bohemia." One is not the same as the other, and the local paper is a better picture of the reality. Both of them attribute her with being a founder of the Dill Pickle Club, which she was certainly present, and took part of.

A July 19, 1940 article titled "A Feather from the Molted Left Wing"[4] in the *Chicago Tribune* tells a plausible story about the gradual disappearance of the shop:

> Phyllis and Geraldine Udell were hawking pacifist literature on the streets during World War I, when other girls of their

---

1 There is no connection to the national chain of stores named "Waldenbooks", though the latter was started in Connecticut in 1933 as "Walden Book Company" and in 1981 became the first bookstore to have a store in every state.

2 Theron's widow Lenetta "Netta" M. Cooper, who was involved in the Labor Defence Council, had worked at Waldens at Plymouth St. location and opened a new bookstore in 1932 at the University Club on S. Michigan Ave named the Concord Book Shop. It later merged with Main Street book store on N. Michigan Ave in 1953. For many years she worked as a talent scout for Harper & Bros., which is now HarperCollins.

3 *The Rise & Fall of the Dil Pickle Club* (Chicago, Charles H. Kerr)

4 Strangely, it was signed "Archie the Cockroach II", a reference to the brilliant (and recommended) satirist Don Marquis' famous characters Archy and Mehitabel.

age were playing hopscotch. Between them and their mother they hatched a plan for putting on dramas of social significance. A stage was set up in the rear of the bookshop and, as the audiences grew, the shop was pushed out of the way until it occupied little more than a window space.

Phyllis eventually married a man named George Hanson and was still directing plays into the 1940's with the Douglas Smith Players, an acting group for youths funded by the Douglas Smith Foundation.

Geraldine had been the personal assistant to Harriet Monroe for a decade until her death in 1935, and became the Business Manager of *Poetry*.

In 1948, the poet Kenneth Rexroth published a poem titled "A Christmas Note for Geraldine Udell." The poem itself mentions recalling Geraldine in a play he refers to as *Gas*, and her performance as the "heroine on the eve of explosion." The first four lines contain a tribute to radicals who spent time at the bookstore: "Debs, Berkman, Larkin, Haywood, they are dead now."

In 1950 Karl Shapiro became editor of *Poetry* and his first decision was to fire "Gerry" Udell.[1]

A PLACE FOR THEIR STORY

As a bibliophile with a passion for fringe literature, discovering the history of this Chicago bookstore, barely mentioned in modern work, was personally fulfilling. The stories that unfolded there and the ripples that undulated from its impact overlap and intermingle with others studied by the Union of Egoists project.

Lillian Udell herself deserves a dedicated study. The blind, erudite woman standing for herself, her family and her passions is too romantic a story to merely be contained in the history of her bookstore and theater. The family and their bookstore demonstrably had an impact on the wider culture, politically, artistically and intellectually.

While there may be more to learn about the Udell's and their store, I hope this first history serves as a beginning for that, and an informative aside for those studying the lives and deeds of the many figures that walked in and out of the doors of that Radical Book Shop.

---

1   *Dear Editor: A History of Poetry in Letters* edited by Joseph Pariri and Stephen Young (New York: W.W. Norton & Company, 2002)

An American Anarchist
Lillian Hiller Udell (1914)

Into every generation are born certain personalities that have the gift of attracting vast multitudes within their orbit, dominating them, animating them with a single purpose, directing them to a common goal. There are other personalities more richly gifted, of more extended vision, who nevertheless live and die unknown to the greater number of their contemporaries. Aristocrats of the mind, these latter disdain to practice the arts by which popularity is gained and held. They attract, but do not seek to dominate. They persuade, but never command. Their passion is without hysteria; their moral indignation is without personal rancor. They cherish ideals, but harbor no illusions. They will gladly surrender life itself for an idea, but they will not shriek for it. Our popular leaders are not seldom led by those who seem to follow. These others advance alone. If they are followed it is without their solicitation. To say that the individualist writer and lecturer whose collected writings are now before us was such a personality may seem exaggerated praise. If so, I have no apology to offer. I only ask that, until you have read the lectures, poems, stories, and sketches which this book contains you will suspend judgment.

Voltairine de Cleyre belonged to the school of thinkers that has suffered most from the misrepresentations and misunderstanding of the unthinking crowd; the school which numbers among its adherents men like Stirner, Ibsen, and, in some aspects of his teaching, Nietzsche; the school that sees hope of social regeneration only in the sovereignty of the individual and the total abolition of the state. She belonged to it because she was at once logician and poet, with a temperament abnormally rebellious against tyranny and an imagination abnormally responsive to every form of suffering.

It has often been remarked that anarchism takes root most readily in those minds that have endured most oppression. Thus Russia, the home of absolute political despotism, is also the birthplace of Bakunin, Hertzen, Kropotkin, and Tolstoy. In America, where what Mencken calls "the new puritanism" operates more oppressively than political government, it is in behalf of sex freedom that most frequent and vehement protest is heard.

In the case of Voltairine de Cleyre this reaction declared itself neither because of political nor of sexual restraint. It came about in the realm of religion. It began from the moment when, at the age of twelve, the sensitive gifted girl was placed in the hands of a Roman Catholic sisterhood, presumably that her education might be safe. For four years the young Voltairine lived at the convent of Our Lady of Lake Huron at Sarnia, Ontario, heartsick with loneliness, writhing under the padded yoke of conventual discipline, gathering within her soul that flame which was never destined to be quenched save in death. Out of that experience she came with a mind wholly emancipated from the dogmas of religion. Not long afterward she entered upon what promised to be a brilliant career as a secularist lecturer.

That a nature like hers would long confine itself to labor in the barren field of theological controversy was not to have been expected. She was too vital, too human. It is possible that the delicacy of her own health intensified her sense of the world pain. Her sympathies are not alone of the intellect but of the nerves. One feels the nerve torture of an imaginative and poetic invalid in her confession of the reasons which had drawn her to adopt the anarchist propaganda. She pictures herself as standing upon a mighty hill from which she writes:

> I saw the roofs of the workshops of the little world. I saw the machines, the things that men had made to ease their burden, the wonderful things, the iron genii, I saw them set their iron teeth in the living flesh of the men who made them; I saw the maimed and crumpled stumps of men go limping away into the night that engulfs the poor, perhaps to be thrown up in the flotsam and jetsam of beggary for a time, perhaps to suicide in some dim corner where the black surge throws its slime. I saw the rose fire of the furnace shining on the blanched face of the man who tended it, and knew surely, as I knew anything in life, that never would a free man feed his blood to the fire like that.
>
> I saw swart bodies, all mangled and crushed, borne from the mouths of the mines to be stowed away in a grave hardly less narrow and dark than that in which the living form had crouched ten, twelve, fourteen hours a day; and I knew that in order that I might be warm—I and you, and those others who never do any dirty work— those men had slaved away in those black graves and been crushed to death at last.
>
> I saw beside city streets great heaps of horrible colored

earth, and down at the bottom of the trench from which it was thrown, so far down that nothing else was visible, bright gleaming eyes, like a wild animal hunted into its hole. And I knew that free men never chose to labor there, with pick and shovel, in that foul, sewage-soaked earth, in that narrow trench, in that deadly sewer gas ten, eight, even six hours a day. Only slaves would do it.

I saw deep down in the hull of the ocean liner the men who shoveled the coal—burned and seared like paper before the grate; and I knew that "the record" of the beautiful monster, and the pleasure of the ladies who laughed on the deck, were paid for with those withered bodies and souls. I saw the scavenger carts go up and down, drawn by sad brutes and driven by sadder ones; for never a man, a man in full possession of his selfhood, would freely choose to spend all his days in the nauseating stench that forces him to swill alcohol to neutralize it. And I saw in the lead works how men were poisoned, and in the sugar refineries how they went insane; and in the factories how they lost their decency; and in the stores how they learned to lie; and I knew it was slavery made them do all this.

And against such slavery this young Amazon of the spirit (for at this time, 1887, she was only twenty-one) declared a life-long warfare. In so doing she separated herself from those who would otherwise have been her natural allies and cut off those opportunities for worldly success which must in the ordinary course of things have come to her.

Finding the cause of economic slavery not in capitalism, as do the socialists, but in the government of man by man through which capitalism is made possible, she was isolated still further from her contemporaries. Hence the obscurity in which her life was passed. Hence the fact that until her death in 1912 she lived quietly, teaching English to the newly-arrived immigrant, scattering about her the treasure of a richly-stored mind as freely as the south wind scatters the perfume it has gathered from the garden in its path. If she had lived nearer to the plane of the generally accepted culture Voltairine de Cleyre might have gained a recognized place among the foremost women of her time.

As it was she gave us in her lectures, now for the first time offered to the public, the most comprehensive exposition of philosophical anarchism that has appeared since the days of Proudhon and Stirner.

Revolutionary Essays
Lillian Hiller Udell (1914)

Has Socialism a literature? This word "literature" is obviously not meant to be used here as a synonym for printed matter, as we speak of the literature of an anti-tuberculosis campaign or a vice crusade. One regrets the poverty of language which forces us to employ one and the same noun in describing the tragedy of an Aeschylus or an Ibsen and the report of a garbage inspector. Socialism has its men of science like Enrico Ferri, its philosophers like Dietzgen, its economists like Marx and Engels, its scholars like Kautsky and Ward, its men of action like Bebel, Haywood and Debs.

In the present inquiry we refer to the art by which noble thought finds adequate expression on the printed page, the medium through which aesthetic or heroic emotion becomes articulate for our own and succeeding generations.

For existence, even our present existence under the wage system, has its aesthetic and heroic phases. None of us should forget that, least of all the pioneers in a revolutionary movement. Granted that the philosophies of the eighteenth century did not take the Bastile or achieve the cataclysm of '93, none the less their work stands as the best inheritance of their time, none the less their writings form the source of highest inspiration for their spiritual descendants of the twentieth century. What we of today are striving for is not merely physical well being, nor even physical well being plus a most intimate and accurate knowledge of our descent from the amoeba and our kinship with the chimpanzee. Does the Socialist movement as at present constituted afford us those elements of poetry and eloquence which nerve the spirit for the great act of rebellion which must precede the bringing in of a better order of things?

One recalls Oscar Wilde's *Soul of Man Under Socialism* and William Morris' *News from Nowhere*. These two master artists have, however, given us pictures of society in its ultimate perfection. Their prophecy is derived less from science than from faith. Mr. Shaw has treated current problems with a lucidity and brilliancy unsurpassed by any contemporary writer. But his appeal is never to the deeper emotions of his readers.

These thoughts occurred to me as I laid down a little volume entitled *Revolutionary Essays in Socialist Faith and Fancy*,[1] by Peter E. Burrowes.

I cannot claim for this author a very high place among literateurs, yet in his best moments he is reminiscent of Carlyle, of Whitman and curiously enough of Friedrich Nietzsche.

At his worst he is mystical even to the point of becoming unintelligible. There is much in these essays that could have been omitted. Yet the reader who can enter into the mood in which the work is conceived will find himself abundantly repaid for the effort. There is throughout all these reflections a fine enthusiasm which acts upon one as a tonic. There are moments of passionate eloquence, almost of poetry. There is little that is dull. One feels that the man who penned them had the temperament of a poet. He is religious, but his religion is of this world. He writes:

> Oh, he is a very present, very near and dear God—the God whose new name I whisper to thee, Socialism. And as you think of the glistening morning thoughts, wherewith so often he has coronated your brow, that crown of yours, which is in the thought world as a rich rose giving out of its folds delightful particles of fragrantly blessed fancies you know nevermore aught of the terrible nearness of God. He is no longer that awful live eye which the priests pulled out of a socket and set staring at you from the altar, staring in among your poor little heart thoughts, to shrivel you up with a horrible fear of God and make you slaves. The God of humanity is so sweetly near, and you so sweetly fearless of his nearness are, that you would if you could, let him into your bosom's heart to stay among the red pulses.

Yet this dreamer is far indeed from holding the point of view of the Christian Socialist. He is never more vehement and perhaps never clearer in his utterance than in his attack upon organized religion:

> There is no vision that ever came to man so unconquerably true as the Socialist perception that the church in every nation is but the voice of the economic ascendant. In America, many are puzzled to see mercantile Protestanism and mercantile infidel-

---

[1] Published by Charles H. Kerr & Company, Chicago, cloth, $1.00, postpaid.

ity flirting so incontinently with Rome. The daily press, which is indubitably run and written by trade and for trade only, cannot nevertheless conceal, and cannot hold back the daily interest of its proprietors in the prosperity and doings of that venerable hypnotist, the approved handmaiden and willing paramour of all despotism, the Roman Catholic Church. And let it be known that she deserves their confidence and affection, for she has never yet officially betrayed any property class, and indeed cannot, for every cell and tissue of her canons, doctrines, and practices was formed in the bowels of riches for its own defense and comfort against the sinners who must work and who do not work enough.

And later:

I do not single out Rome by name in order to separate her dishonorably from the other churches of the world. Her own claim that in Western lands she is the mother church is sound; she is older and wiser in the police business than her Protestant progeny, who though a bit naughty in the past, are filially imitative. It was but a minor property quarrel that separated them, the major property interest of uniting against Socialism will soon bring them all together again. Hence the billing and cooing between their eminences in the press and the priesthood.

The so-called progressive movement in modern capitalist politics will find here little encouragement:

The reform tinker, who has no higher aim in politics than to mend the passing pots, we do not endorse. He shall pass through life mending pots, and shall leave the world with yet more pots to mend than he found there when he came.

We are to have no illusion concerning the depth of our slavery to those who own the tools of production:

This parasite class, according to the observed law prevailing in all ages, having obtained control of the economic needs and forces of their time, 'clothe themselves with authority, and gird themselves with the powers of the state. They therefore can supplement the privation by exclusion from the means of living. They can also add positive suffering to the negative misery they can beat you by all the rods of law into their laboratories; they can entangle your feet in every step you make for freedom; they can not only use the guns of the state against you but they can force you to use them against yourself; they can by possessing all the archives, know how much it is costing you to live, and can, as private employers, cut your wages down to that. From the signal boxes of the state they know your incoming and outgoing. They can control your mind; they can go behind you and before/and float over you, and build military tunnels under your feet with your own hands. You cannot be emancipated while that class is in control and they can afford to let you play at all kinds of radical discontent as long as you leave them where they are.

And oh, the contempt he pours upon the middle class:

> The middle class man is the negative, empty space between two facts, he is nothing—not even a hypocrite. He has no role to play anywhere in any great world. No great social movement is for him who is but a soaker, maintaining himself by keeping on the moister side of everything.

That which is of value in these essays is a certain power born of earnest conviction which meets Tolstoi's test of art, viz., that the emotion of the writer is communicated to those who read. They are not literature, it is true, but they deserve to be read.

Three Tributes to Georgia Replogle
(Various) (1904)

GEORGIA REPLOGLE,
Anarchist, Atheist, Materialist, Freelover and Beautiful Soul.
DIED, DENVER, COLORADO, OCT. 22, 1904.
DEDICATED to HENRY REPLOGLE.

∉

The doors have opened, they have shut,
And thro' their valves our friend has gone;
A gentle woman, brave and straight,
A friend to be depended on.
Life is a mystery to all,
The strangest part of life is death,
But deem you then that all is done
Because the lungs no more have breath?
But she was wise and she was sweet,
And, whether death be death or no,
She lived a life worth while and great,
And that is why we loved her so.

∉

IN MEMORIAM.

Georgia E. Replogle passed into the unknown Oct. 22. Her life was a beautiful one, and despite the years of illness she never lost her beautiful character, her superb charity and patience. *Lucifer* readers are numerous who knew her well; they will feel the loss as much as can be.

Her funeral was a beautiful one: her dear friends said the things they thought, read her favorite selections, sang her songs.

Now that it's over, that Our Georgia sleeps forever in the cemetery—under a beloved elm tree—where the mountains keep a vigil—we who remain have nothing left but the memory of her who lived so well, so beautifully. She cherished her friends —she loved nature, her life was a poem—to emulate her would be farcical—to remember her as she was is our boon.

Many who see this will say, "Dear Georgia," and, after all is said and done, can any better tribute be offered?

B. F. BRUKK.

∉

It is with a feeling of sadness for myself and for all who loved and needed "Our George," and yet with joy for her release from her long agony, that I give to our readers the news of the death of Georgia Replogle. She was one of my earliest and dearest friends; one who had a very great Influence on my life. She was one to whom, as a young girl, I could talk of my hopes, ambitions, as I could to no one else—one with whom I could "think aloud." Many years have passed since we parted, but it has seemed good to know that she lived and that I had her sympathy and her love. And now—well, she is released from her suffering, and I know that if conscious existence continues, her true, loving spirit is the same.

Her enthusiasm for her work was so great that she ignored her physical needs, working long and steadily, with insufficient care for herself. The result was that she has been an invalid for many years, though continuing to work as long as was possible to do so. Everything that could be done by her friends for her relief was done, but without avail—so now the end has come. A biographical sketch will probably appear in our next issue.

L. H.

Three You Cannot Afford to Do Without
Trevor Blake (2019)

Three identical advertisements for *The Eagle and the Serpent* from three different periodicals. The address 26 Clovelly Mansions was used by *The Eagle and the Serpent* Volume 2 Number 5 (September 1902), edited by John Erwin McCall and Malfew Seklew. It was also the address of John Basil Barnhill and for Sophie Leppel. So many names for so few authors! Malfew Seklew seasoned his *Gospel* with health advice, and one wonders if Sophie Leppel was, like McCall, another name for the work of Barnhill.

> THREE MAGAZINES YOU CANNOT AFFORD TO DO WITHOUT.
>
> **Nationality.**
>
> Advocates the Dismemberment of Large Empires and the Multiplication of Small Nations.
>
> **The eagle and the serpent.**
>
> An Organ of Emersonian Egoism. A Journal for Free Spirits and for Spirits struggling to be Free.
>
> **Life and Beauty.**
>
> A magazine which instructs its readers how to be their own doctors. In its columns the leading actresses and authors tell how they keep young and beautiful.
>
> **Samples of these 3 magazines for 10 centimes.**
>
> Address, *Life and Beauty*, 26 Clovelly Mansions, Gray's Inn Road, London W. C., England.

Freedom by Helen Wilmans (Sea Breeze). Volume VIII Number 44 (April 17 1901), Volume VIII Number 45 (April 24 1901), Volume VIII Number 48 (May 1901)

> **THREE MAGAZINES YOU CANNOT AFFORD TO DO WITHOUT.**
>
> NATIONALITY—Advocates the Dismemberment of Large Empires and the Multiplication of Small Nations.
>
> THE EAGLE AND THE SERPENT—An Organ of Emersonian Egoism. A Journal for Free Spirits and for Spirits struggling to be Free.
>
> LIFE AND BEAUTY—A magazine which instructs its readers how to be their own doctors. In its columns the leading actresses and authors tell how they keep young and beautiful.
>
> Samples of these three magazines for 12 cents, United States Stamps. Address, LIFE AND BEAUTY, 26 Clovelly Mansions, Gray's Inn Road, London, W. C., England. apr 13-3mo

Revue franco-allemande / Deutsch-franzosische Rundschau by M. Henry / F. A. Lattmann (Berlin). Number 53 (May 1901), Number 54 (June 1901), Number 56 (August 1901), Number 57 (September 1901)

> **Three Magazines You Cannot Afford To Do Without.**
>
> **NATIONALITY.**
> Advocates the Dismemberment of Large Empires and the Multiplication of Small Nations.
>
> **THE EAGLE AND THE SERPENT.**
> An Organ of Emersonian Egoism. A Journal for Free Spirits and for Spirits struggling to be Free.
>
> **LIFE AND BEAUTY.**
> A magazine which instructs its readers how to be their own doctors. In its columns the leading actresses and authors tell how they keep young and beautiful.
>
> SAMPLES OF THESE THREE MAGAZINES FOR 12 CENTS U. S. STAMPS.
>
> Address, LIFE AND BEAUTY, 26 Clovelly Mansions, Gray's Inn Road, London, W. C., England.

Now by Henry Harrison Brown (San Francisco). Volume II Number 1 (March 1901)

HUMANITY FIRST LETTERHEAD
JOHN BASIL BARNHILL (CIRCA 1919)

The letterhead used by John Basil Barnhill (aka John Erwin McCall, editor of *The Eagle and The Serpent*) for his journal *Humanity First* (1919).

Ernesto A. Longa's *Anarchist Periodicals in English Published in the United States (1833-1955)* gives the following of the journals' Prospectus:

> Humanity First is trying, in the spirit of John Ruskin, to remove the fundamental injustices which breed class hatred. We hold that unless Privilege is curbed, red ruin will inevitably overrun the world. We stand for the abolition of interest and all the privileges, of which it is the direful spring, and it seems to us that thus and thus only can society evolve, in a peaceful and orderly manner, to its next stage. Privilege and Humanity cannot co-exist.

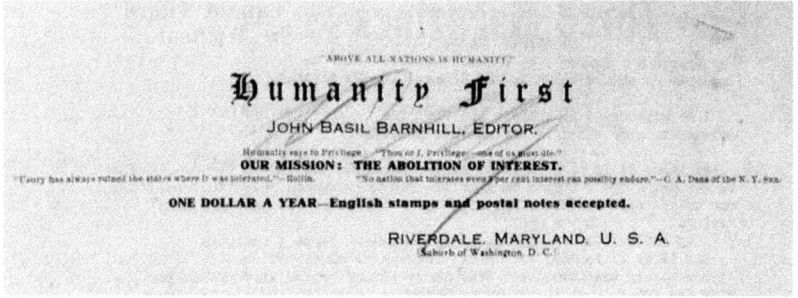

The letterhead reads:
"ABOVE ALL NATIONS IS HUMANITY."
Humanity First
John Basil Barnhill, Editor
Humanity says to Privilege "Thou or I, Privilege: –one of us must die."
OUR MISSION: THE ABOLITION OF INTEREST
"Usury has always ruined the states where it was tolerated." –Rollin
"No nation that tolerates even a per cent interest can possibly endure." –C.A. Dana
of the N.Y. Sun.
ONE DOLLAR A YEAR–English stamps and postal notes accepted.
Riverdale, Maryland, U.S.A.
(Suburb of Washington, D.C.)

THE MAN BORN BLIND
AMBROSE BIERCE (1888)

A man born blind received his sight
   By a painful operation;
And these are things he saw in the light
   Of an infant observation.

He saw a merchant, good and wise.
   And greatly, too, respected,
Who looked, to those imperfect eyes,
   Like a swindler undetected.

He saw a patriot address
   A noisy public meeting.
And said: 'Why, that's a calf, I guess,
   That for the teat is bleating.'

A doctor stood beside a bed
   And shook his summit sadly.
'O see that foul assassin!' said
   The man who saw so badly.

He saw a lawyer pleading for
   A thief whom they'd been jailing,
And said: 'That's an accomplice, or
   My sight again is failing.'

Upon the Bench a Justice sat,
   With nothing to restrain him;
'Tis strange,' said the observer, 'that
   They ventured to unchain him.'

With theologic works supplied,
   He saw a solemn preacher;
'A burglar with his kit,' he cried,
   'To rob a fellow creature.'

A bluff old farmer next he saw
   Sell produce in a village,
And said: 'What, what! is there no law
   To punish men for pillage?'

A dame, tall, fair and stately, passed,
   Who many charms united;
He thanked his stars his lot was cast
   Where sepulchers were whited.

He saw a soldier stiff and stern,
   'Full of strange oaths' and toddy;
But was unable to discern
   A wound upon his body.

Ten square leagues of rolling ground
   To one great man belonging,
Looked like one little grassy mound
   With worms beneath it thronging.

A palace's well-carven stones,
   Where Dives dwelt contented,
Seemed built throughout of human bones
   With human blood cemented.

He watched the yellow shining thread
   A silk-worm was a-spinning;
'That creature's coining gold.' he said,
   'To pay some girl for sinning.'

His eyes were so untrained and dim
   All politics, religions,
Arts, sciences, appeared to him
   But modes of plucking pigeons.

And so he drew his final breath,
   And thought he saw with sorrow
Some persons weeping for his death
   Who'd be all smiles to-morrow.

Joel's Literary Corner
Carlo de Fornaro (1911)

Illustration by Carlo de Fornaro (1871 - 1949) from *Mortals and Immortals* by Carlo de Fornaro (New York: The Hornet Publishing Company, 1911). Seen here are the habitués of Joel's Cafe, pre-Volstead, members all of the literary circle Benjamin DeCasseres was part of for many years.

From left to right: Michael Monihan (Publisher of *The Papyrus*, a splinter of Elbert Hubbard's Roycrofters), Leonard Charles Van Noppen (poet, literary expert, and translator), Edwin Markham (poet), Booth Tarkington (Pulitzer Prize-winning novelist), Benjamin DeCasseres (writer) Shaemas O'Sheel (poet), (upper right corner) and Joel Rinaldo (restaurateur).

The caption reads "Joel's Literary Corner; once Mexican Revolutionary Table." Benjamin DeCasseres moved to Mexico in 1906 to work with Sunday-editor Carlo de Fornaro at El Diario, an English-language newspaper. Political turmoil in Mexico caused DeCasseres to return to New York, bringing Fornaro with him.

In a biographical sketch of DeCasseres published in *Arts & Decoration* (Vol. 22 No. 3, January 1925), Fornaro wrote:

> Once DeCasseres was assigned to review a gala bull fight, the corrida of which contained fifty thousand spectators. The article was so brilliant and so Hugoesque in its fantasy that the next day a committee of literati of the capital came in a body to honor him and thank him for it. "Never," they declared, "had any Spanish or Latin-American author written such stupendous stuff." On his return to Manhattan he assisted the ex-Sunday editor of El Diario to write "Diaz, Czar of Mexico," an arraignment of the existing régime and a prophecy of the revolution. Within two years the political storm swept from power the whole crew of tyrant greasers and grafters.

From DeCassere's preface to *Mortals and Immortals*:

> The caricaturist has that touch of the satanic in him which redeems him from the pestilential morality and sanity of the work-a-day world. He is impersonal, disenchanted, a Nietzschean. That satanic touch which lies at the basis of his art is something akin to that cold, intellectual smile that Iago threw on the corpses of Othello and Desdemona.

Poems from the Imp
Benjamin DeCasseres (1916-1921)

The Sun, Sunday, 16 Jan. 1916
THE MYSTERIOUS WEAVER

Time the weaver of life,
Time the unraveller of death
Is busy a-weaving across the seas
A monstrous Rune
To the rhyme of a croon
That wells from the Londons of the dead.

∉

The Sun, Sunday, 13 Feb. 1916
W.S.: 1616-1916

You are not buried where your body lies,
Where matter and the worms hold long carousel
But there, atop the catafalque of Night,
Where Aldebaran has beatified your soul with light,
You await the magic touch of the eternal Prospero.

∉

The Sun, Sunday, 26 March 1916
ACROSS THE GULF

The smooth white bellies of sharks.
Thunder clouds on the horizon like giant murder masks.
Perfumes from the undiscovered isles foundered in immeasurable depths,
The eternal shambles of the spaces,
The perpetual moan of the sea deep dead,
And our three brains from the captain's bridge laying siege to the fortified mysteries of God!

Harrisburg Star-Independent, 11 Sept. 1916
MORNING MAGIC

Away! Away!
The hour is struck
On the golden tocsin over the hill
Day is dawning
The flush of the morning
Mantles the dale and fires the rill!

Away! Away!
Night is fled
Into its cellar down in the West,
The dew is a-gleaming,
Broken the dreaming
Of the lark in the hollow and the bird in its nest!

Away! Away!
Alborak is waiting
For my chimeric flight to the Ulbra Place.
Ere the new light dies,
Ere the morning flies
His hoofs will flash in the Night of Space!

Don Marquis' Column, *The Washington Times*, 8 Dec. 1916, p. 10
RUINS

His eyes like two frozen seas epitomized and locked in horizons of flesh,
His frigid brow like the high scroll of Eternity (that enormous minute that has no seconds),
His impervious dreams
And inviolable visions
A set and fixed ruin on the scoff of his lips—
He, the Poet, Vulcan of the exquisite, like an unsigned and desolate god awaited the inexorable minute of putrefaction.

The Sun, 7 July 1918, Sec. 6 p. 7
TO A GREAT AMERICAN

Halloo! Halloo! Walt Whitman—
Wherever you are—
There in the rich sun soaked earth of your beloved
 America,
Or there in the light and scream of a comet,
Or deep in the heart of Our Boys that march with
 banner and sword and song
'Gainst the rotten old dynasties of Europe—
Your America is born! Sleep no more, great prophet
 of us, bold, gray trumpeter of our destiny.

Halloo! Halloo! Old Walt!
Tremendous visionaries of these your States,
Chanter in flame-swept strophes of the Super-Race
 of the West
That was to scale the last wall of feudalism—
We salute thee, there in your tomb where the Delaware waters swash and murmur,
We, your America, born of your vision, accoutred
 for the Sublime Adventure,
Are waiting to clasp *you*, Homer to our unborn Saga!

Halloo! Halloo! gray-bearded god,
Encloser of us, womb of our destiny—
The strongest man in the world,
America,
Is to take for bride the most beautiful woman in the
 world,
France.
Priest of that wedding, come back like an avatar, as
 you promised,
Come back to the altar of your beloved,
Old Walt of Camden, America incarnate, Shakespeare of Patriots, King David of Democrats!

Bloomington Indiana Daily Student, 19 July 1918
FRANCE
(1789-1918)

France, of genius the mother;
France, to all me a brother;
France, that the Hun seeks to smother—
    Hold a little while!

Souls of many made one,
Pleiades become as a sun,
Miraculous men of Verdun—
    Hold a little while!

Supermen on the Aisne,
Mothers from Var to the Seine,
Workers from Brest to Lorraine,
    Hold a little while!

Torn and bleeding and battered,
Tricolor riven and tattered,
Rheims and Lens gasping and shattered—
    Hold a little while!

Mystical daughter of d'Arc,
Hugo of the Promethean spark,
Shall France go down in the dark?—
    Hold a little while?

Gods out of dreams are they,
Cyclops of an ancient lay,
The truth, the life and the way—
    Hold a little while!

A Giant across the sea
Is coming to set thee free
Or coming to die with thee—
    Hold a little while!

Judge, 23 Aug. 1919, Vol. 77 No. 1975, p. 7
THE DREAM POCKET

I am a tobacco pouch,
Stuffed with a thousand dreams,
Heavy with the magic of reverie.

My shredded treasure is more potent
Than the Seven-Leagued Boot
Or the hat of Fortunatus.

I am the little Castle of Memory and Hope,
The lotus-leaf for the Mouth of old King Care,
The amber pool where poets fish for images.

I am your old tobacco pouch.

Don Marquis' Column, *The Washington Times*, 7 Feb. 1917, p. 6
THE RISEN GIANT!

Like the pounding of vast thundercloud waters
'Gainst the mountains and cliffs that circle the world,
The footsteps of a giant, weary of insult, are heard in the West!

His hair is unkempt, but his eyes are like unto
Two conflagrant suns set in the head of the demi-god Hercules
As he strides from the Sierras to the peaks of the East to meet the
    Sultan of Hell!

Now the ears of a world stand a-prick and a-wonder
As against the westering spaces rises the avenger
Clad in muscle and anger.

And there is heard in the night the furious death-croak
Of the tired black eagles of Prussia
That roost in the helmet of the Sultan of Hell!

Harrisburg Telegraph, 12 Sept. 1921, p. 10
TO THE OLD SOAK

I am the Mecca of Sorrows,
The blenched and frozen cheek
On which all tears fall,
The Night unto which
All secret sighs are uttered—
Yet, to-day, I am a Mansion of Revels,
A Hall of Laughing Echoes,
A Mirthful Prometheus—
For a case of Scotch hath been bootlegged unto me
This day!

II.

Man—
Having arrived at mental maturity,
Deciphered all Babylonian bricks,
Cuneiform inscriptions and the Congressional Record,
Having explored the air, the earth,
The sea and the Poles,
Having stacked up billions of books
On oodles of subjects
(Saying nothing of canvas and stone
And Victor Herbert),
Having struck the condor and the eagle with panic,
And printed electric words on the air—
Having done all this and a pile of other things,
In his infinite ennui,
He nuzzles into my hip pocket!
Fantastic Man!

Life, 21 Sept. 1916, Vol. 68 No. 1769, p. 477
STAR-DUST AND NETTLES

LOGIC is the bones of the mind; dreams are its flesh and blood, its face and feet—and wings.

Happiness is the art of making yourself believe that you will some day be happy.

The secret of the Great Man is to strike down the people with a terrible truth and raise them up with a dazzling lie.

The universe is a visible unnecessary point moving toward an invisible necessary end.

Geniuses are those insane angels who chant their peans in the iron cells of Reality.

There is no maniac comparable to a reformer.

The brain of the philosopher is the real City of Magnificent Distances.

Veneration is the fossil of an extinct enthusiasm.

Without doubt motion is impossible.

Desire has to-morrow for its empire; possession has yesterday for its kingdom.

When we speak of women we are either satyrs or asses. All women know this.

The Altruists' Corner
*Trevor Blake &
Kevin I. Slaughter* (2019)

"Egoism is the law of the ego" said Malfew Seklew. Egoism is a description of what I do, not a prescription of what I should do or a prohibition against what I should not do. Egoism is no more the cause of my ego than Newton's laws are the cause of motion. I am the territory and egoism is the map. Only as it serves me does it matter to me whether anyone is or is not an egoist. One simply does not recruit or exile oneself. Not this One, anyway.

My draw to egoism is the high degree it places on the descriptive over the prescriptive. It has an internal consistency that no other philosophy has. Far more than A = A, I = I. To avoid confusing the territory and the map, it is good for me to avoid overly promoting egoism as 'something other people should do.' It serves me that people purchase print from the Union of Egoists, and I do not advocate egoism as a cause. It is also good for me to keep an eye on the critics, who might catch my strong hand saluting a flag instead of patting myself on the back.

"The Altruists' Corner" is a regular column in *Der Geist*, consisting of a chronological catalog of critics of egoism. The votes are in, and nearly everyone hates The One. Egoism is too far left, too far right, too far outside and too self-centered - or so call the causists. Original spellings retained to honor and to shame.

The Religion of the Future by Edward von Hartmann.
Translated by Ernest Dare. London: W. Stewart & Co. 1886. Page 84.

The reader may compare Max Stirner's work, *The Individual and His Property* (*Der Einzige und sein Eigenthum*, Leipzig, Wigand, 1845), especially the chapter, "Humanitarian Liberalism" ("Der humane Liberalismus"). This book, richer in ideas than the complete works of many a celebrated philosopher, is, in the carnival-like extravagance of its thoroughly logical conclusions, the most strikingly unintentional proof of the impossibility of making Individualism the basis of

Morality, and of the necessity of finding this basis in Monism. There has been a conspiracy of silence against this book even in the most liberal circles, and people have covered their faces with virtuous indignation at it. But the secret terror, betrayed by this mode of action, only proves that they have not been able to find a weak point in this unpleasant adversary, or that they have shrunk from putting on the only weapons with which this egoism can be struck to the heart, namely, Monism and Pessimism.

∉

"Anarchism Kills Individualism" (uncredited)
in *Freedom* Volume 1 Number 1 (October 1886) page 3.

"Individualist Anarchism" is a round square, a contradiction in set terms. As a cube is not a ball, so "Individualism" is not Anarchism. *What, then is Individualism*? It is the chaos of to-day in social and industrial life, which has sprung from the licentious play of self-will. Self-will is the will to be somewhat, and to have hold and sway something in isolation from other such wills, and in opposition to them. Property, domination, government, law, are embodiments of this self-will. Individualism is this striving, grabbing, over-reaching, and self-seeking of atoms, that seek to possess human individuality, but go about their quest in the wrong way. It calls itself civilization, progress, fair competition, free trade, and many other fine names. It is, in reality, internecine war and suicide. The kick-and-catch-and-keep-who-can hurly-burly of a Rugby football match is not a picture of true Society. A mob is not Society; its irrational and self-thwarting movements do not constitute social conduct. [...] There is no real living and fruitful I, apart from Thou and You. Personality implies communion. The individual implies the commune. These are mutually sustaining and inclusive. Is it because Anarchists see with both eyes solidly; it is because they are not blind to the two-foldedness of the fact of human life in union, that they are sometimes obliged to free themselves from the charge of "individualism?" If so, it is evident that it only requires a rightly distinguishing mind to clear them.

"The Egoist" by Ivan Turgenev. Uncredited translation from *Freedom* Volume 1 Number 9 (June 1887).

He possessed everything necessary to render him the scourge of his family.

He came into the world healthy and rich—and healthy and rich he remained during the whole of his long life. No offense was ever brought home to him; he committed no fault whatever either in word or in deed.

He was of stainless character. And proud in the consciousness of his character, he pressed with it everyone to earth—relations, friends, acquaintances.

His character was to him capital. And with this capital he dealt at usurious interest.

This character gave him the right to be pitiless, and to do nothing beyond the good ordained by law.

And pitiless he was, and did no good. For benevolence prescribed by law is not benevolence.

He never paid the slightest regard to any but his own so perfect person; and he became seriously angry when others were not equally zealous in caring for him.

However, he did not regard himself as an Egoist; and there was nothing he more bitterly condemned and pursued than egoism and egoists. And this was natural, for the egoism of others stood in the way of his own.

Knowing himself to be free from the slightest weakness, he could neither understand nor tolerate the weakness of others. Indeed, he understood nothing and no one, for on all sides, above and below, in front and behind, he was surrounded by his own personality.

He did not even understand what it was to forgive. To himself he had forgiven nothing; why should he need to forgive another?

Before the judgment-seat of his own conscience, before the countenance of his own god, this miracle, this monster of virtue, raised his eyes towards heaven, and with firm, clear voice exclaimed "Yes, verily, I am a worthy and a moral man."

These words he will repeat on his dying bed; and even in the supreme moment nothing will be affected in that heart of stone—in that heart without fault or stain.

O vileness of self-conscious unbending, cheaply-bought virtue? Art thou not more hateful than the open vileness of vice?

∉

Ezekiel Slabbs in *The Firebrand* Volume 1 Number 2
(Portland: February 3 1895).

"*Solidarity*, the organ of the Communists, has reappeared under the editorship of J. H. Edelman, who expects to issue it semi-monthly." - *Liberty*. *Solidarity*, the organ of the COMMUNIST-ANARCHISTS, comrade Tucker. The followers of *Liberty* have no monopoly on the title anarchist; all of us are not philosophers. Please remember that in the future.

∉

"Books, Reviews and Magazines" (uncredited).
To-Morrow Volume 2 Number 2 (February 1906) p. 84

"The Philosophy of Egoism," by James L. Walker (deceased), is unquestionably a masterpiece of clear thinking, and for pure English, deftly and effectively applied, is pre-eminent. But with the highest regards due the deceased author's work, now made public, we suggest that the "philosophy" implied in the title is not more than an individual conception of the word egoism. The entire work is given to correct defining of words rather than to the intelligent interpretating of *life*.

∉

"Zerschagt die konterrevolutionären schwarzen rattenfänger."
Agit 883 Issue 37 (October 23rd, 1969) page 4.

Die Haschrebellen sind ebenfalls Leute dieses Schlages. Im Munde führen sie Mao Tse-Tung und im Herzen tragen sie die ideologischen Hintertreppenautoren Bakunin, Stirner etc. Früher besaass der Anarchismus eine Vertbindung zum Proletariat, or repräsentierte de kleinbürgerliche Fraktion des Proletariate. Heute sind die Anarchisten völlig vom Proletariat abgeschnitten. Sie versuchen deshalb über ihre wahren Ziele hinwegzutäuschen und langfriatig mit der persöhnlichkestozerstörenden Suchtuitteln Opium und Heroin sich die Von der revolutionären Bewegung gewonnen Jungen Genossen willfahrig zu machen.

[The Hash-rebels are also people of this type. In their mouths they have Mao Tse-Tung and in their hearts they have the ideological back-stairs authors Bakunin, Stirner, etc. In the past, anarchism had an attachment to the proletariat, or represented the petty-bourgeois faction of the proletariat. Today the anarchists are completely cut off from the proletariat. Therefore, they try to hide their true aims and, in the long run, to make the young comrades won by the revolutionary movement complacent, with the help of opium and heroin, with which they destroy themselves. - Trevor Blake, translation]

∉

Letter to the Editor by Bunn Nagara from *Freedom*
Volume 42 Number 4 (February 27th, 1981).

Unless the Stirnerian becomes a hermit, his philosophy cannot be sincere and practicable at the same time. To live in society, one's philosophy and practice need to be workable and durable - which is obvious enough. [...] I know one or two people who come in the 'Stirnerian mould' - outspoken, critical, loud, but whose social-political thoughts have not progressed very far. [...] Stirner remains at the starting-post a pouting adolescent defiance, with no tangible pathways for realizing his ideals. It is not Proudhon or Kropotkin or Morris then who is abstract or religious, but Stirner himself who is being fervently utopian, a personalist fundamentalist. What would stop his "association of egoists" from exploiting one another and everyone else? Would they want to stop themselves from doing so?

... and from Graham Baugh...

S. E. Parker's insane paeans to Stirner and egoism give *me* no pleasure (and if I were an egoist that would be the only criticism possible). But besides being boring and banal, Parker's platitudes are replete with falsehoods. [...] I find egoists calling themselves anarchists a curious thing (and not because I'm a naive social utopian). If all that is important is myself and my desires, why should I oppose all authority? Obviously I won't oppose my Own authority, as I can use my power to make others conform to my will, to satisfy *me*. And if other authorities work to my advantage the egoist thing to do would be to support them also. If I were an egoist I would much prefer to be a master than a slave, but I wouldn't be opposed to slavery.

∉

"All things are Nothing to Me / Stirner's Communism" by Jacob Blumenfeld. Historical Materialism Conference, New York, 14–16 January 2010.

Max Stirner is no historical materialist and yet here I am, writing a paper on Stirner's communism. What motivates this gesture? [...] The difficulty we are coming across is that the nothingness of the ego which Stirner describes as the condition of the unique can be seen from a Marxian perspective as either a description of the essence of capital or a description of the essence of the proletariat–the class which has no particular qualities, but only the generic form of labor-power. How is this possible? Well, is it not so different a structure than Hegel's *Phenomenology of Spirit* or Marx's *Capital*? In the *Phenomenology*, the movement of Spirit can be seen either from the perspective of Substance or of Subject, and the "we" of the text is nothing but the mutual constitution of the two. In Marx's *Capital*, the structure of capitalism is seen from both the perspective of capital and labor, and capitalism is nothing but the mutually constitutive relation of the two. For Stirner, the movement is between the ego and its own, or better yet, the unique and its properties. Communism or Egoism is not the privileging of one side over the other, but the abolition of the separation between the two from within the negative potential of one. Subject negates and realizes substance, the unique negates and realizes property, the proletariat negates and realizes capital. [...] When society or community becomes the privileged form of the individual's self-relation, then the task of the unique is to desecrate the community as much as possible. Yes, capital desecrates the world, wastes and squanders it. But the unique doesn't retreat in the face of this, rather they out-desecrate, out-waste, and out-own capital. The communist subject that is produced in such activity is not some Nietzschean *ubermensch*, but what

Stirner calls an *Unmensch*, an un-man, one who's being is indifferent to the formal structures which seek to capture it, classify it, identify it, work it.

∉

THE EMPLOYERS' ASS., AND THE UNION SHEEP.
(Desmond as Cow-Boy, at the City Hall on Friday evening last.)

RAGNAR REDBEARD

Arthur Desmond was born in 1859. As a young man he was a vital force in Antipodian radical politics. He was an advocate of autonomy for the Maori people. He was a member of the Active Service Brigade, a theosophy-socialist labor union. He wrote and published anonymous and pseudonymous essays and poetry critical of banking and organized religion. When he vandalized a bank with a sticker reading "gone bung" (suggesting the bank was about to collapse) he was subject to arrest and found it expedient to leave the Southern Hemisphere.

Desmond landed first in London, where he published a series of pamphlets under the title *Redbeard's Review*. He then relocated to Chicago, Illinois, where he would live the remainder of his days. In 1896 he wrote an expanded version of *Survival Of The Fittest* (an essay from his time in Australia) and combined it with *Women And War* and published it as *Might is Right*.

Might is Right was repeatedly reprinted during the author's lifetime. It was wildly popular among radicals and revolutionaries, many of whom lived in Chicago. Redbeard served for a time as co-editor of the egoist journal *The Eagle and The Serpent*, and for a time he shared a Chicago address with Sirfessor Malfew Seklew.

Desmond, meanwhile, worked in an ice cream and candy factory. It was there he met his wife, the mother to his son Arthur Konar Desmond. After his confectionary days, and after his wife left him, he opened Thurland and Thurland, a bookstore. He quietly sold books until his death in 1929.

Illustration of Arthur Desmond from the New Zealand *Observer*, Volume X, Issue 623, (December 6th, 1890). The caption reads: "The Employers' Ass, And The Union Sheep. (Desmond as Cow-Boy, at the City Hall on Friday Evening Last.)"

Ragnar Redbeard and the I.W.W. 163
Trevor Blake   *(2019)*
A terrific and exhaustive study revealing a deep connection between Redbeard and the Chicago workers union.

"Might is Right" Cartoon 189
Punch   *(1853)*
Predating the release of the book by that name.

Ragnar Redbeard in the Berkeley Barb 190
Trevor Blake   *(2019)*

Three from Reedy's Mirror 191
(various)   *(1917)*

Commentary On Redbeard in Reedy's Mirror 198
Trevor Blake   *(2019)*

Arthur Desmond Satirized in New Zealand Observer 201
(uncredited)   *(1890)*
Full page illustration and caption from *New Zealand Observer* Volume X, Issue 624 (December 13th, 1890). "Christ as Social Reformer" is an article he wrote for the journal *Zealandia*.

House of Gowrie Advertisement 202
Arthur Desmond   *(N.D.)*

Ragnar Redbeard and the Industrial Workers of the World
Trevor Blake (2019)

> My property is not a thing, since this has an existence independent of me; only my might is my own. Not this tree, but my might or control over it, is what is mine. Now, how is this might perversely expressed? They say I have a right to this tree, or it is my rightful property. So I have earned it by might. That the might must last in order that the tree may also be held—or better, that the might is not a thing existing of itself, but has existence solely in the mighty ego, in me the mighty—is forgotten. Might, like other of my qualities (humanity, majesty, etc.), is exalted to something existing of itself, so that it still exists long after it has ceased to be my might. Thus transformed into a ghost, might is—right.
> —Max Stirner, *The Ego and His Own*
> (New York: Benjamin R. Tucker, 1907)

INTRODUCTION

Ragnar Redbeard (1859–1929), author of *Might is Right*, stands alone. His book was famous during his lifetime, but he elected to never draw attention to the man who wrote it. He wrote a book on the sovereignty of the individual that is worthy of sharing a shelf with Max Stirner or Friedrich Nietzsche. *Might is Right* is a book of blood and thunder, written by a man whose day job was in an ice cream factory. In 2019, Underworld Amusements published *Might is Right: The Authoritative Edition*. This is the edition to buy.

The Industrial Workers of the World (the I. W. W., "the Wobblies") is an international organization founded in 1905 in Chicago, Illinois. The Preamble to their Guiding Principles and Rules is little changed since that time:

> The working class and the employing class have nothing in common. There can be no peace so long as hunger and want are found among millions of the working people and the few,

who make up the employing class, have all the good things of life. Between these two classes a struggle must go on until the workers of the world organize as a class, take possession of the means of production, abolish the wage system, and live in harmony with the earth.

The Wobblies have improved the working conditions in many factories, shops, mines and other worksites all across the world. In their struggle to achieve their goals, hundreds of Wobblies have been fired, blacklisted, tortured, imprisoned and lynched. They also published dozens of newspapers and magazines. The I. W. W. exists today. Find a branch near you, read their tremendous back catalog of publications and find out more about this significant and fascinating organization, the "one big union."

Ragnar Redbeard spoke poorly of the "dignity of labor." He wrote that organizations were fit for sheep, and that the only moral role was to be a butcher or a wolf among them. The Industrial Workers of the World spoke highly of the working class. They wrote that it was inherently immoral as well as ineffective to separate workers into competing individuals or competing unions. It might seem that there could be no harmony between them.

This essay is an overview of a time when the Wobblies were enthusiastic supporters of *Might is Right*.

The editors of *Der Geist* are not advocates. We do not deign to define what is or is not egoism, we only publish what was said to be egoism in print between the years 1845 and 1945. Any reader who wishes to be told what is "real" egoism is compelled to read elsewhere. Further, the editors of UnionOfEgoists.com and *Der Geist* do not invest a single word or thought toward who the "real" Wobblies were or are. Any reader who wishes to form such an opinion is encouraged to both read about IWW history and to meet with current members of the Industrial Workers of the World.

The Wobblies of a century ago took pains to differentiate themselves from both the left and the right. They mocked (and sometimes fought) both communists and the Ku Klux Klan. In advocating for industrial organization, they refrained from unionizing any individual shop or industry. The Wobblies of today are not the Wobblies of a century ago. Today's Wobblies do align themselves with the left, and do unionize individual shops and industries. The book *Might is Right* of a century ago delivered pains to the left and the right. It mocked (and sometimes most cruelly) both labor and religion. In advocating for 'the just' it refrained from identifying who that might be outside of 'the strong.' Due to a bowdlerized edition of *Might is Right* published in a small edition the 1960s, the book came to be commonly associated with right-leaning groups. Those who are familiar with only today's I. W. W. may find it strange that at one time a number of their most active members were enthusiasts for *Might is Right*. Those who are familiar with only the common association of *Might is Right* with right-leaning groups will find it strange that at one time it was championed by the Industrial Workers of the World.

For the last time, the editors of UnionOfEgoists.com and *Der Geist* will remain eternally mute when it comes to "real" egoism and the "real" I. W. W. We only provide quotes and context from the past, when the two walked shoulder to shoulder.

∉

RALPH CHAPLIN

Ralph Chaplin (1887–1961) was the author of the lyrics to "Solidarity Forever," an anthem of the Industrial Workers of the World. He drew the black cat logo used by the I. W. W. He was put off by the failure of Soviet Russia and did his part to keep communism out of the I. W. W. In 1917 he was sentenced to twenty years in prison for conspiracy to hinder the draft. Chaplin quotes a criticism of *Might is Right* in his autobiography *Wobbly: The Rough-and-Tumble Story of an American Radical* (Chicago: The University of Chicago Press, 1948):

> One day [prison guard Captain Eddy] found a copy of *Might Makes Right* [sic] in our cell. He picked it up with a grimace. "Is this a Wobbly book?" The question was directed at Dan Buckley, who explained that it had been written a quarter of a century previously by one "Ragnar Redbeard," a diminutive, repressed Near North Side philosopher with delusions of grandeur. "Well, I've noticed a lot of Wobblies reading the damn thing. Let me have it." Captain Eddy read *Might Makes Right* through. Then came the expected outburst. "This tinhorn 'superman'—this crummy, gutter-spawned, half-pint dictator, yammering about the 'might of the proletariat!'"

He continued: "Let's be honest about the thing. A lot of you so-called 'rebels' would be failures under any kind of social order. Some of you guys blame capitalism for the things God neglected to give you. Wage slaves, bah! You wouldn't be wage slaves if you had what it takes to be anything else. Take it from the Marines, the 'Ragnar Redbeards' of the world can be handled with a fly swatter, if it ever comes to a showdown!"

Ralph Chaplin and the I. W. W. were the ones reading (if irreverently) *Might is Right*, while the prison guard with a military background was the one damning it.

∉

MORTIMER DOWNING

Mortimer Downing was the spokesperson for a number of Wobblies called the "Silent Defenders." In 1919 he was sentenced to ten years for 'conspiring to oppress employers of labor.' Downing had this to say to the Court: "Only one generous, kindly doctrine ever came into the world, only one that will put individual responsibility where it belongs. That is the doctrine that might is right." In the company of so many other Wobblies speaking of *Might is Right* as a book they read and advocated, it is difficult to think of Downing's phrase as only a coincidence.

∉

THE ONE BIG UNION MONTHLY

The *One Big Union Monthly* was a magazine published by the Industrial Workers of the World initially edited by John Sandgren.

In *The One Big Union Monthly* Vol. I No. 1 (March 1st, 1919) a direct if uncredited quote from *Might is Right* appears in the form of a comic illustration on page 10 (see facing page).

An essay titled "Might is Right" in Vol. 1 No. 4 (June, 1919) does not mention Redbeard by name, but includes this passage suggesting a familiarity with Redbeard's view:

Capital and Labor Are Partners—Not Enemies

John D. Rockefeller, Jr.

Uncredited quote from *Might is Right* from *The One Big Union Monthly* Vol. I No. 1 (March 1st, 1919).

> Ideals are pale things in this world of cold, ruthless materialism. Idealism in politics never was. We, who are revolutionists, know that the crimes of the age will only be ended by Might. The criminals of this age who have written the Paris treaty, will only be mastered by those who are economically stronger. All the ideals in the universe will not budge them. But a class organization will sound their doom. Labour must fight capital by the same weapons. They on top and we below—both are materialists. We want the world, not because we love justice, but because we love ourselves. We fight revolutions not for Idealism but for self-interest. Such is the law of life. Why, like Wilson, pretend that it is otherwise. The power of the I. W. W. comes from our realization of this materialism. We are not fogged by illusions of right and wrong. We do not bow at the shrine of tender phrases.
>
> Might is right. Let us learn the lesson, and organize until we are the mightiest.

A familiarity with Redbeard's views is also shown in "Courts and Direct Action" in *One Big Union Monthly* Vol. 1 No. 7 (September 1919):

> The truth may be a fine thing and it is said that it will prevail, but it must have "power" behind it, for Might is Right, as it has been and will continue to be.

Redbeard was acknowledged by the Wobblies by name in *One Big Union Monthly New Series* Vol. II No. 1 (January 1938):

> Stars and suns may perish
> Empires wax and wane
> But the law of struggle
> Eternal shall remain.
> Ragnar Redbeard

As late as February 1938, *One Big Union Monthly New Series* (Volume II Number 2) was making references to "Sainted Redbeard."

The *One Big Union Monthly*, published by the Industrial Workers of the World, both quoted Ragnar Redbeard's book *Might is Right* and incorporated his ideas into their own.

∉

THE INDUSTRIAL PIONEER

The Industrial Pioneer was a publication of the Industrial Workers of the World edited by Henry Van Dorn. In Volume I No. 2 (June 1923) there is a poem by Ragnar Redbeard:

> The Logic of To-Day
> Then what's the use of dreaming dreams—that "each shall get his own"
> By forceless votes of meek-eyed thralls, who blindly sweat and moan?
> No! A curse is on their cankered brains—their very bones decay:
> Go! Trace your fate in the Iron Game, is the Logic of To-day.

Once again, a publication of the I. W. W. devotes its resources to citing Ragnar Redbeard and *Might is Right*.

∉

DIRECT ACTION

Direct Action was a Wobbly newspaper from Sydney, Australia. In Vol. I No. 1 (January 31st, 1914) it published "Might is Right" by Covington Hall, based on a poem by Ragnar Redbeard in *Might is Right*. The poem by Hall was quoted again in Vol. I No. 5 (May 15th, 1914). In Vol. 2 No. 28 (May 1st, 1915) *Direct Action* published the Redbeard original. *Direct Action* Vol. I No. 16 (November 1st, 1914) published a column of "Redbeardisms" made up of direct quotes from *Might is Right*. *Direct Action* Vol. 3 No. 62 (March 18th, 1916) again published the Redbeard poem "Might is Right." Several issues in Volume 3 of *Direct Action* announced a book of poems including "Might is Right," including No. 56 (February 5th, 1916), No. 59 (February 26th, 1916), No. 61 (March 11th, 1916), No. 64 (April 1st, 1916) and No. 65 (April 8th, 1916).

E. A. Griney wrote an essay titled "Might is Right" for *Direct Action* Vol. 3 No. 91 (October 7th, 1916). This essay claims that violence justifies itself in the triumph of those who use it well, be they capitalists or Wobblies:

> It is highly amusing when we hear the workers indulging in sentimental wailing and gnashing of teeth at the candidness of speech of some undiplomatic employer or the harshness of the measures used by the employing class to beat the working class into subjection. [Property owners are] justified in using any and every means to suppress manifestations of working-class discontent. A strike being an attempt to defy the rights of capitalists to exploit labor for profit must be crushed without mercy. [...] The morality of [strike breaking] is quite in keeping with all the theory and practice of our present social system. We must give the employing class credit for their splendid organization and solidarity when faced by an active revolt of wage slaves. It is for the latter to learn and profit by example. When they are capable of practicing similar solidarity they will conquer their masters, and the power of their might will be proof of their right.

This same issue quotes from the individualist essay "The Right to Ignore the State" by Herbert Spencer, reprinted in a limited edition by the Union of Egoists in September, 2017. *Direct Action* Vol. 3 No. 104 (January 13th, 1917) published an essay claiming it is not violence in itself that is wrong, but the monopoly on violence held by the State. James Pope, in "Demand an Answer," dismisses thought over action and writes that when the workers take up violence it will, by that very act, become morally correct. In other words, might is right.

> [We] are living in a mad world at present, but the only answer the lords and rulers have is: "Might is Right, we have the might and if you dare to enlighten this 'dumb terror,' we will deal with you as we have already dealt with thirty members of your class." [...] That is the answer the "boss" makes to the questions. You philosophers and sentimentalists may rave about ethics and justice until Doomsday, but until you develop the might to threaten his position he will continue to be right.

Pope also wrote "The Justification and the Objective of the I. W. W." for *Direct Action* Vol. 4 No. 123 (May 26th, 1917):

> To-day the workers co-operatively run industry. The Capitalist is nothing but the extractor of surplus profits of industry. Organized industrially, the worker would be the greatest power on this earth, and the happiness of society as a whole comes before the greed of a class. Might is right: so what's the matter with the workers owning the tools of production?

Direct Action Vol. III No. 94 (October 28th, 1916) expressly links the Industrial Workers of the World to the ethics of Ragnar Redbeard in the poem "The Stalwards of Gaol" by C. D.:

> Fellow slaves, line up to-day
> The war is on in fierce array
> The weapon you must use to fight
> Is "One Big Union"—"Might is Right"

Direct Action Vol. 2 No. 29 (May 15th, 1915) publishes "The General Strike," a play in rhyming couplets by S. W. which concludes: "There is only one alternative in sight / We must confess the truth— that Might is Right." The contradictions of Redbeard's ethics (it sure doesn't feel right to be on the receiving end of might) are acknowledged in *Direct Action* Vol. 1 No. 19 (December 15th, 1914) in "What My Environment Causes Me to Believe" by W. H. Lewis: "Might is Right, even though it be wrong."

In *Direct Action* there is support for the claim that *Might is Right* was read and respected by the international body of the Industrial Workers of the World. *Direct Action* quoted Redbeard, paraphrased Redbeard and wrote original texts inspired by Redbeard.

∉

THE INDUSTRIAL WORKER

The Industrial Worker was a newspaper published by the Industrial Workers of the World. The *Industrial Worker* Vol. 2 No. 27 (September 24th, 1910) published the poem "Might is Right" by "Author Unknown." And Vol. XIV No. 110 (February 21st, 1933) published

"Without Strong Union Script and Peonage are Miner's Reward" by 4. M. J., which concludes: "The master class have never been known to give anything. If we expect to improve our lot, we will have to organize and fight. Might is right. Get busy."

The Industrial Worker is another Wobbly newspaper that shows the influence of Ragnar Redbeard and his book *Might is Right*.

Left to Right: Jay Smith, E. F. Doree, Covington Hall, C. L. Filigno.

∉

COVINGTON HALL

Covington Hall (1871–1952) was the primary editor and contributor to an I. W. W. newspaper first published as *The Lumberjack* and later as *Voice of the People*. He wrote for *One Big Union Monthly*, *The New Solidarity*, *Direct Action* and other Wobbly newspapers and magazines. Hall published books of poetry and essays including *Battle Hymns of Toil*, *Dreams & Dynamite*, *Labor Struggles in the Deep South* and *Songs of Rebellion*. A biographic sketch of Hall appears in *Battle Hymns of Toil*:

> For more than forty years he has been active as a writer, speaker and publicity agent in many fights made by the Workers and Farmers for economic freedom. He has fought

with them in Louisiana, Texas, Arkansas, Oklahoma, Oregon, North Dakota, South Dakota, Florida, and all over Dixie. He began this activity as a follower of William J. Bryan. He has taken an active part in many strenuous political campaigns, such as the Farmers' Non-partisan League of North Dakota, where, in 1920 and 1921, he acted as one of the publicity chiefs for the League under Governor Frazier and his Attorney General, now Congressman William Lemke. [...] He has written thousands of poems in defense of and to stir up the Farmers and Workers everywhere. These poems have gone all over the English speaking world and many have been translated into other tongues. Always, even when they were merely propaganda verse, the purpose has been to call the Workers and Farmers to battle for the Brotherhood for which the Rebel Carpenter of Nazareth fought and died. These poems have not been written to please those of us who might be timid or hold fixed prejudices.

Covington Hall received the praises of labor leader Eugene V. Debs, labor cartoonist Art Young and wrote under the names Covington Hall, Covington Ami, Covami, Notgnivoc, and Voc the Barbarian.

The Lumberjack was published in Alexandria, LA and New Orleans, LA. *Voice of the People* was published in New Orleans, LA and Portland, OR. Hall served as editor for all but the final nine issues, which were edited by B. E. Nilsson. Three issues of the newspaper were numbered "27," and the newspaper volumes were numbered first I, then II, then III, then back to II. To lessen confusion, citations made here refer to an absolute sequence printed on all issues, numbers 1 through 97.

The first words on the first page of the first issue of *The Lumberjack* are "MIGHT IS RIGHT." These words appear in the masthead of every issue, nearly one hundred in total. Reverence for Redbeard is found throughout *The Lumberjack / Voice of the People* across the years of its publication, in every location it was published and by every editor that published them.

Issues 49 through 53 of this Wobbly newspaper contained variations of this advertisement for *Might is Right*:

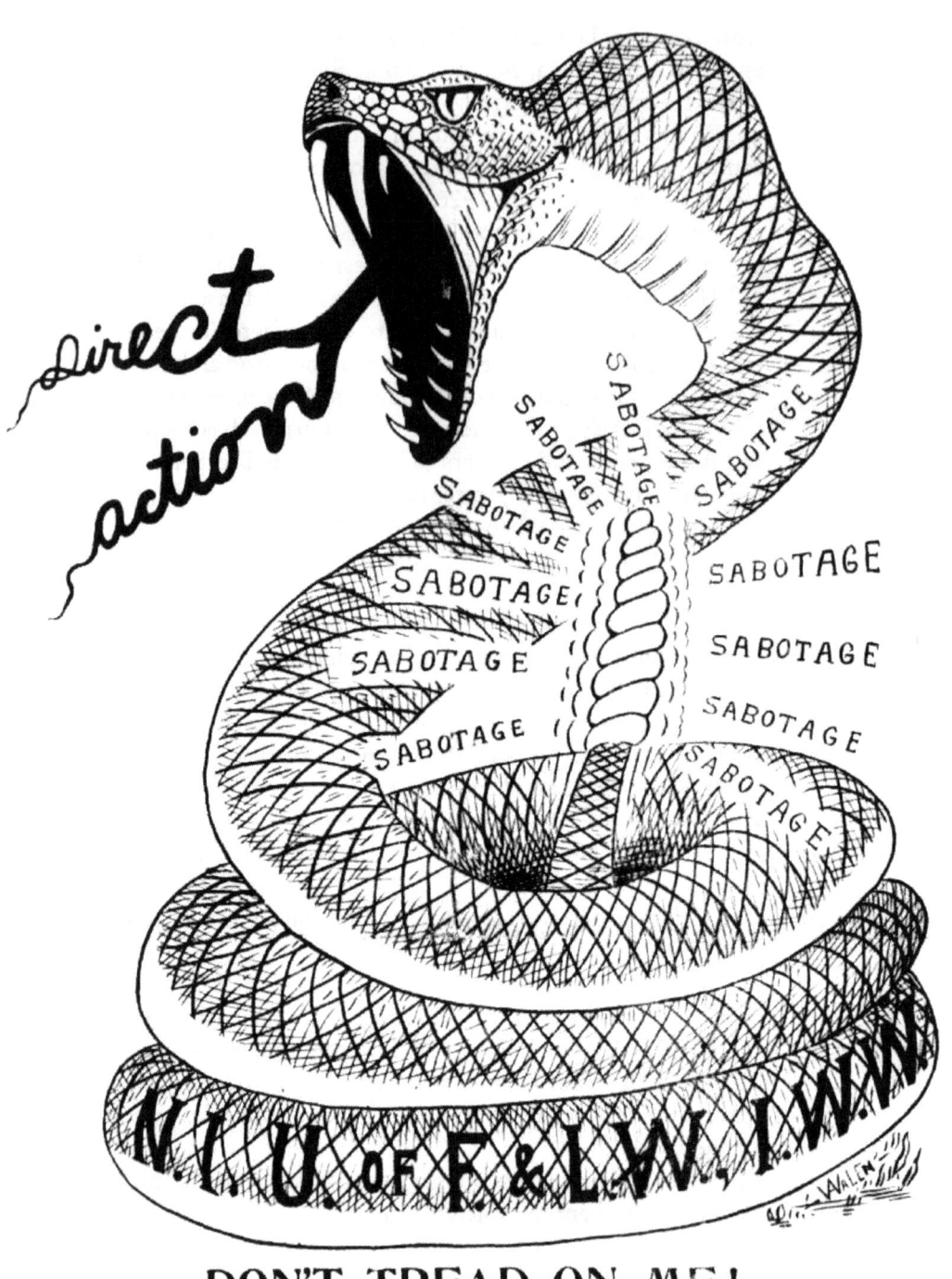
Image Caption

Might is Right.

Have you read that great book, "Might Is Right" by Ragnar Redbeard? You will not agree with all he speaks, but, he will make you THINK—think outside the beaten sheep-paths. You will, probably, gag at this:

"'He fed the hungry'—but to what end, I say? Why should a famishing multitude be fed by a god? And that, too, in a land said to be flowing with milk and money [sic]! Would not such a mob be far better dead? Would not Napoleon with his cosmic 'whiff of grape-shot' be just the right man for such an occasion? From the harmonious nature of things, it is clear that men were intended to feed themselves by their own personal exertions or perish like dogs. He therefore who 'feeds the hungry' is really encouraging poltroonry (which includeth all other crimes) FOR MEN WHO QUIETLY STARVE WITHIN REACH OF ABOUNDING PLENTY ARE—ALL POLTROONS... They waste their lives pursuing shadows; and for hire build their own tombs. Their minds are below freezing point, nay! below zero! Crippled souls are they.

"Courage, I say! Courage that goes its way ALONE, as undaunted as when it marches to 'victory or death' amid the menacing stride of armed and bannered legions. Courage, that never falters—never retreats! That is the kind of courage the world lacks today... That is the kind of courage that has never turned a master's mill. That is the kind of courage that will never turn it. That is the kind of courage that will DIE, rather than turn it."

If you want to read this tremendous Epic of the Strong, send us a DOLLAR and we will send you a copy of "MIGHT IS RIGHT" and THE VOICE for 30 weeks; or we will send you the book alone for FIFTY CENTS. Address THE VOICE, 520 Poydras Street, New Orleans, LA.

Issues 54 through 56 of this Wobbly newspaper contained variations of this advertisement for *Might is Right*:

Might is Right

"What," says Redbeard, "is your 'civilization and progress' if its only outcome is hysteria and downgoing?

"What is 'government and law' if their ripened harvests are men without sap?

"What are 'religions and literature' if their grandest productions are hordes of faithful slaves?

"What is 'evolution and culture' if their noxious blossoms are sterilized women?

"What is education and enlightenment if their dead-sea-fruit is a catiff race, with rottenness in their bones? ...

"In this arid wilderness of steel and stone I raise up my voice that YOU may hear...

"Courage, I say! Courage that goes its way ALONE, as undaunted as when it marches to 'victory or death' amid the menacing stride of armed and bannered legions. Courage, that never falters—never retreats! That is the kind of courage the world lacks today... That is the kind of courage that has never turned a master's mill. That is the kind of courage that will never turn it. That is the kind of courage that will DIE, rather than turn it."

"Might is Right" is published in England and is out-selling any book we ever handled. Better order a copy to-day.

If you want to read this tremendous Epic of the Strong, send us a DOLLAR and we will send you a copy of "MIGHT IS RIGHT" and THE VOICE for 30 weeks; or we will send you the book alone for FIFTY CENTS. Address THE VOICE, 520 Poydras Street, New Orleans, LA.

Issues 57 through 72 of this Wobbly newspaper contained variations of this advertisement for *Might is Right*:

Might is Right

The root-thought of "Might is Right" lies in this quotation: "Property, remember, is an integral part of freedom and manhood. They who have no property are at the mercy of those who have. Woe unto him who has 'nothing.' Economic dependence is a flaming hell."

> If every Lumberjack, Worker and Working Farmer in the South would read this great book they would clearly see how they have lost their inheritance in their native land by themselves losing the old-time fighting spirit of the Clansmen.
>
> You will not agree with all Redbeard says no more than I do, but YOU should read this extraordinary book. One thing it will do—it will show you how the "Mighty" rule and rob and proletarianize the race and then, it is up to you to THINK FOR YOURSELF.
>
> If you want to read this tremendous Epic of the Strong, send us a DOLLAR and we will send you a copy of "MIGHT IS RIGHT" and THE VOICE for 30 weeks; or we will send you the book alone for FIFTY CENTS. Address THE VOICE, 520 Poydras Street, New Orleans, LA.

Issues 71 through 80 of this Wobbly newspaper contained variations of this advertisement for *Might is Right*:

> "Might is Right." Send us $1.00 for FOUR 13-week or TWO 26-week PREPAID Subcards and we will send you a copy of this great "gospel of the strong." FREE. The book alone is 50 cents.

Readers of this I. W. W. newspaper took advantage of the Wobbly's offer of *Might is Right*, as shown in letters to the editor.

> Issue 66
>
> Enclosed please find 50 cents for which send me "overs" each week for five weeks, you may string them out 10 weeks if you want to. "Might is Right" received O. K. and it sure is a humdinger, never read anything like it before; it is something I needed to understand years ago. A. J. Sulem, Rialto, CA

> Issue 67
>
> Fellow-worker Voice: Find enclosed Post Office Money Order for two bucks. One buck put to the bucking of capitalism—maintenance Fund of the Voice; for the other buck please send me two of the books "Might is Right" and I will help to buck the present order of society by the aid of "Redbeard." I have one copy of the Doctor's fiery spirit and am getting it

worn out by others reading it, and I want to have one copy on me always. There is something the matter. The capitalists, master class, are stupid or depend on the stupidity of the working class to keep themselves in power. Every slave should read "Might is Right" once, twice, and then three times. I. J. Blocer

Issue 71

Enclosed you will find $2.00 for which send one copy of "Might is Right" and the balance in three months' subs, and oblige. Wm. Lorwe.

Issue 72

So, workers of the world, UNITE, and become our fellow-workers by joining the IWW, the ONE BIG UNION based on scientific principles, having its roots deep down now already in the economic field [...] Remember this, that everything on this earth has been and is now and will always be gained by MIGHT. It's might that rules the universe and it's might that survives in the struggle for existence. Remember, MIGHT IS RIGHT. Yours for the revolution, T. G. Gaveel.

Issue 81 is the first issue published in Portland, Oregon. This and all remaining issues retain "MIGHT IS RIGHT" in the letterhead, but issues 81 through 84 contain no other mention of Ragnar Redbeard and his book. It might be thought that the editor had a change of heart regarding Redbeard along with a change in location. The newspaper also had a change in editors, with final nine issues edited by B. E. Nilsson. The evidence is that except for four out of ninety-seven issues, the Wobblies consistently promoted Ragnar Redbeard and his book *Might is Right*, because he returns to their pages from issue 85 onward. Nilsson attended an October 1st, 1914 lecture by Dr. Charles C. Chapman in Portland Oregon, and reported that Dr. Chapman included Ragnar Redbeard in his lecture on "The New Evolution."

The Industrial Workers of the World published Ragnar Redbeard in their newspaper *The Lumberjack / Voice of the People*:

Issue 51

"There is no dignity in a bent back—no glory in a perspiring brow—no honor in greasy copper-riveted rags. There is nothing very delectable in picks, shovels, and calloused paws. 'Dignity of Labor!'—Dignity of hell!

'Cursed is the brow that sweats—for hire, and the back that bends to a master's burden!"—from *Might is Right*

Issue 53

Life is strife for every man, For every son of thunder; Then be a lion, not a lamb, And don't be trampled under. Redbeard

Issue 53

HATE FOR HATE
AND RUTH FOR RUTH. EYE FOR EYE
AND TOOTH FOR TOOTH. SCORN FOR SCORN
AND SMILE FOR SMILE. LOVE FOR LOVE
AND GUILE FOR GUILE. WAR FOR WAR
AND WOE FOR WOE. BLOOD FOR BLOOD
AND BLOW FOR BLOW! Redbeard

Issue 61

Behind all Kings and Presidents, all Governments and Law,
Are army corps and cannoneers to hold the world in awe;
    For Might is Right when empires sink in storms of steel and fame,
And it is right when weakling breeds are hunted down like game. —from *Might is Right*

Issue 78

Owners are Freemen; the Propertyless are Slaves.

Issue 86

From the falls of St. Lawrence to wide Amazon
From Clye and from Shannon to Danube and Don
    From the Nile and the Ganges to rolling Hoang-Ho—
It's "woe to the vanquished" wherever you go.
    From the icefields of Klondyke to Kongo's dark stand
From the geysers of Heckla to red Rio Grande
    From the banks of the Tiber to fair Caliao—
It's "woe to the vanquished" wherever you go.

                                       Ragnar Redbeard

Issue 95
Always think your own thought
All other thoughts reject;
Learn to use your own brain
And boldly stand erect
Redbeard's Review London 1901

The Industrial Workers of the World also published works inspired by Ragnar Redbeard in *The Lumberjack / Voice of the People*. Issues 69, 71, 77 and 78 published variations of Redbeard's poem "The Logic of To-Day" as found in *Might is Right* (albeit with the following note from editor Covington Hall: "We have taken the liberty to arrange this great poem in the way we believe it should flow"). Hall's version was also published in *The Labor Journal* (Everett, Washington, March 14, 1913) and *Freedom's Banner* (Iola, Kansas, July 5th, 1913). Issue 87 published a column of "Redbeard-Isms" that quote from *Might is Right* with one interesting addition. "Even as I write (1890–1896)—with wrecked civilizations lying around me, cold and chill—outraged nature is preparing her whirlblasts of wholesale avengements." The two dates in parenthesis do not appear in the original. This suggests a familiarity with not only the contents of *Might is Right* but also its publication history. Here are more examples of work by the Industrial Workers of the World that are paraphrases of or inspired by Ragnar Redbeard...

Issue 3
He who loses is always wrong. [...] Cursed is the job-coward; damned are the meek—Blessed are the strong, for they shall inherit the earth. [...] Might is right, but there is no might where right is not.

Issue 7
Remember: Organization is Power. Might is Right.

Issue 8
There is no RIGHT without MIGHT; no MIGHT without RIGHT!

Issue 15
I repeat: TRUTH conquers all things; MIGHT is RIGHT; ORGANIZATION IS POWER. [...] If you want to get a big-

ger share of what you produce, you must be organized, too. This is not a question of sentiment. It is a COLD SCIENTIFIC FACT. MIGHT IS RIGHT, and today the Bosses have the MIGHT because they are COMBINED TOGETHER for their MUTUAL BENEFIT, which is the exploitation of the wage workers out of whose sweat and blood is wrung the millions which your masters enjoy.

Issue 15

"MIGHT IS RIGHT" the workers say
"Our number is our might;
We're growing stronger every day
And soon will win our fight."

Issue [32]

Real liberty is a conquest, not a bequest.

Issue [33]

The survival of the fittest is the scientific song that regulates the universe and pushes things along; and in the world's class struggle there isn't any doubt but the idle, useless class will some day peter out; this means that only useful folks will finally survive, because no other class is fit to feed and keep alive.

Issue 34

FORCE! Sonny, everything rests on force, and the working class INDUSTRIALLY ORGANIZED, acting as a unit, is the most terrible force than can to-day be brought against the capitalist society.

Issue 45

Of all the old wise saws, that ever saw the light, There is none to be compared to: MIGHT IS RIGHT

Issue 79

Might is Right, but might without right never did, does not, and never will exist.

Issue 97

THE RULES by Peter Bell

> They gathered all in marble hall
> To see which one would rule;
> To the masters they whispered a word or two,
> Then they whispered to the fool,
> "Justice!" he cried; and away he ran
> To boast about his right,
> But the masters jeered as the poor fool cheered,
> For they knew that might was right.
>
> Issue 97
> NOW AND THEN by Peter Bell
> In the primitive jungle dark as night
> The cruel beasts roared in their terrible might
> And the weakest died in a hopeless fight,
> For there in the jungle might was right.
> Now in the jungle of laws and men
> The same is proven time and again,
> And the slaughter feasts on a battlefield
> Only proves that justice to might must yield.
> The Twentieth Century with its laws
> Takes the place of the wild beasts' jaw
> And the facts of life are hidden from sight
> So the workers won't learn that might is right.

Covington Hall also published *Rebellion* ("Made Up of Dreams and Dynamite"). This appeared to be a magazine in support and sympathy with the I. W. W., but Hall's own work rather than that of the I. W. W. itself. Several issues include *Might is Right*. From *Rebellion* Vol. 2 No. 2 (May 1915):

> "The Gospel of the Strong" Have you ever read Ragnar Redbeard's great book *Might is Right*? Well, if you have not, you have missed something worth while. [...] In this great book Ragnar Redbeard boldly asserts that Liberty and true Manhood cannot return to humanity until the World is cleansed by a catastrophic struggle against the "Emperors of Gold" and their "rotting millions." In blazing and thought-shocking sentences he shows the inevitability of what is now going on in Europe and America and calls the "New Nobility" to rise and unslave the Race. If you care to read the books of

men who think and speak their own thoughts, who are not simply human phonographs, send us $1.00 (or in New Orleans and foreign $1.10) and will mail you a copy of *Might is Right*, a copy of the *Songs of Love and Rebellion*, and send you *Rebellion* for 3 months.

The Lumberjack / Voice of the People made reference to Ragnar Redbeard in issue after issue. They also made reference to other egoist and individualist authors. Issue 49 quotes Friedrich Nietzsche: "The State! Whatever the State sayeth is a lie; whatever it hath is a theft; all is counterfeit in it; the gnawing, sanguinary, insensate Monster, it even bites with stolen teeth—its very bowels are counterfeit." Issue 59 quotes Nietzsche: "To injure intentionally when our safety and existence are involved, or the continuance of our well- being, is conceded to be moral." *Rebellion* Vol. 2 No. 2 (May 1915) again quotes Nietzsche: "Far too many are born. For the superfluous ones the State was invented. Behold how it allureth them: how it devours and chews and masticates them!" The following issue of *Rebellion* (Vol. I No. 3, May, 1915) not only repeats the offer for *Might is Right* and *Songs of Love and Rebellion*. *Rebellion* Vol. I No. 7 (January 1916) offers *Might is Right* ("will force you to sit up and think for yourself") and *The Right to be Lazy* (1883) by Paul Lafargue (1842–1911). "You never even dreamed you had such a right, but Lafargue will prove it to you more wittily and logically than a right was ever before set forth." *The Lumberjack* Vol. 1 No. 20 (May 22nd, 1913) includes an essay by George G. Reeve, who sang the praises of Redbeard in two issues of *Ross's Monthly* (March / April 1920; August 1921). *Voice of the People* Vol. II No. 39 (October 2nd, 1913) reprints an essay by individualist and peer of Benjamin Tucker, Jo Labadie. And Issue 59 of *Voice of the People* includes a quote from the primary author of the philosophy of egoism, Max Stirner: "He who has might has right; if you have not the former, neither have you the latter—Stirner."

The poem "I, the Soul" appears in *Rebellion* Vol. I No. 7 (January 1916). It begins and ends:

> There is no earthly power strong enough
> To bar my way. There is no road so rough
> But I will follow to the farthest goal
> Or, failing, fall unconquered—I, the Soul

> [...] My fate it is my own to make or mar
> I am my spirit's good and evil star
> And here, or here after, let come what will
> I am and shall be my own master still.

Rebellion Vol. I No. 9 (March 1916) paraphrases Redbeard on the front cover: "A hymn of praise I raise / A high and holy song / The race IS to the swift / The battle to the strong." *Rebellion* Vol. I No. 12 (June 1916) published the poem "The Supreme Law," which begins and ends...

> The Soul of Man is builded from a trillion years of strife,
> The Iron Law of Struggle is the Supreme Law of Life;
> Thru all, o'er all, it follows man wherever he may range—
> The urge compelling progress and the power forcing change.
> It is the law of being, fixt, immutable and right,
> The essence of eternity, infinity and light;
> All matter, mind and spirit, all is mothered out of strife—
> The Iron Law of Struggle is the Supreme Law of Life.

There is no cause to speculate about what *Might is Right* meant to the Wobbly editors of *The Lumberjack / Voice of the People* because they published their view. From Issue 85...

> *The Voice* has received lately many clippings from Australian papers regarding the life of the strange, wild genius called "Ragnar Redbeard," the author of that harsh yet thought-compelling book *Might is Right*—a book that all rebels will want to read, especially in these days that 'try men's souls' but with the philosophy of which, in full, no social revolutionary will agree. But the book will force you to think and it will show you in naked words how the mighty rule. It is not Redbeard's fault if, as he says, you misunderstand his "meanings."
> It seems that he, "Ragnar Redbeard," was a New Zealander of Irish parentage and, strange as it sounds, for through all *Might is Right* runs vitriolic hatred of the politician, he was one of the organizers of the Australian "Labor Party." It was perhaps the bitter experience he gained in that abortion

that led him to express, in blighting words, the burning contempt of and for politicians that blazes out on every page of his truly great book. It is said of him that he could stand upon a public platform and recite offhand, making up the verses as he went, poems of great strength and beauty. That one of his favorite stunts was unmasking the hypocrisy of the "Christian Church" by dressing himself in rags, walking up the main aisle of a church on a "Lord's Day" and taking a front pew, when, of course, he would be ushered out; that at other times when the spirit was upon him, he would stop and begin a mighty address to some group of workers standing on the street, soon blocking the entire way, when again, of course, "Lawanorder" would be on his back.

From all the clippings, the man is shown in his book—a mighty and terrible hater of all hypocrisy, especially that mother of all hypocrisies and shams, capitalist society. In the last clipping sent the writer thereof closed with the exclamation, "I wonder who killed him!" You will not agree with all this great book teaches but you will never regret reading it. We will send it to you for 50 cents, or send us $1.00 for 13 weeks, or two 26-week prepaid subcards and we will send you the book free.

How the Wobblies viewed the works of Ragnar Redbeard is summed up in Issue 86...

Might is right. Get right, you cuss.

You will not agree with all that the Industrial Workers of the World and *Might is Right* teach, but you will never regret reading about them.

∉

SOURCES
Chaplin, Ralph: *Wobbly: The Rough-and-Tumble Story of an American Radical*. (Chicago: The University of Chicago Press, 1948).
Direct Action Vol. I No. 1 (Sydney January 31st, 1914).
—– Vol. I No. 5 (Sydney May 1st, 1915).
—– Vol. I No. 16 (Sydney November 1st, 1914).
—– Vol. I No. 19 (Sydney December 15th, 1914).

—– Vol. 2 No. 28 (Sydney May 1st, 1915).
—– Vol. 2 No. 29 (Sydney May 15th, 1915).
—– Vol. 3 No. 62 (Sydney March 18th, 1916).
—– Vol. 3 No. 56 (Sydney February 5th, 1916).
—– Vol. 3 No. 59 (Sydney February 26th, 1916).
—– Vol. 3 No. 61 (Sydney March 11th, 1916).
—– Vol. 3 No. 64 (Sydney April 1st, 1916).
—– Vol. 3 No. 65 (Sydney April 8th, 1916).
—– Vol. 3 No. 91 (Sydney October 7th, 1916).
—– Vol. 3 No. 94 (Sydney October 28th, 1916).
—– Vol. 3 No. 104 (Sydney January 13th, 1917).
—– Vol. 4 No. 123 (Sydney May 26th, 1917).
Hall, Covington: *Battle Hymns of Toil*. Oklahoma City: General Welfare Reporter 1945.
—– *Dreams & Dynamite*. Chicago: Charles H. Kerr 1985.
—– *Labor Struggles in the Deep South*. Chicago: Charles H. Kerr 1999.
—– *Songs of Rebellion*. New Orleans: Covington Hall 1915.
Freedom's Banner (Iola, Kansas, July 5th, 1913).
Industrial Pioneer, The Vol. I No. 2 (Chicago June ,1923).
Industrial Worker, The Vol. 2 No. 27 (Chicago September 24th, 1910).
—– Vol. XIV No. 110 (Chicago February 21st, 1933)
Labor Journal, The (March 14th, 1913)
Lumberjack, The 1 Vol. I No. 1 (Alexandria January 9th, 1913).
—– 2 Vol. I No. 2 (Alexandria January 16th, 1913).
—– 3 Vol. I No. 3 (Alexandria January 23rd, 1913).
—– 4 Vol. I No. 4 (Alexandria January 30th, 1913).
—– 5 Vol. I No. 5 (Alexandria February 6th, 1913).
—– 6 Vol. I No. 6 (Alexandria February 13th, 1913).
—– 7 Vol. I No. 7 (Alexandria February 20th, 1913).
—– 8 Vol. I No. 8 (Alexandria February 27th, 1913).
—– 9 Vol. I No. 9 (Alexandria March 6th, 1913).
—– 10 Vol. I No. 10 (Alexandria March 13th, 1913).
—– 11 Vol. I No. 11 (Alexandria March 20th, 1913).
—– 12 Vol. I No. 12 (Alexandria March 27th, 1913).
—– 13 Vol. I No. 13 (Alexandria April 3rd, 1913).
—– 14 Vol. I No. 14 (Alexandria April 10th, 1913).
—– 15 Vol. I No. 15 (Alexandria April 17th, 1913).
—– 16 Vol. I No. 16 (Alexandria April 23rd, 1913).
—– 17 Vol. I No. 17 (New Orleans May 1st, 1913).
—– 18 Vol. I No. 18 (New Orleans May 8th, 1913).
—– 19 Vol. I No. 19 (New Orleans May 15th, 1913).
—– 20 Vol. I No. 20 (New Orleans May 22nd, 1913).
—– 21 Vol. I No. 21 (New Orleans May 29th, 1913).
—– 22 Vol. I No. 22 (New Orleans June 5th, 1913).
—– 23 Vol. I No. 23 (New Orleans June 12th, 1913).
—– 24 Vol. I No. 24 (New Orleans June 19th, 1913).
—– 25 Vol. I No. 25 (New Orleans June 26th, 1913).
—– 26 Vol. I No. 26 (New Orleans July 3rd, 1913).

—- 27 Vol. I No. 27 (New Orleans July 10th, 1913).
One Big Union Monthly Vol. 1 No. 1 (Chicago March, 1919).
—- Vol. 1 No. 4 (Chicago June, 1919).
—- Vol. 1 No. 7 (Chicago September, 1919).
—- New Series Vol. II No. 1 (January 1938).
Oregon Daily Journal (Portland, OR August 30, 1914).
Rebellion Vol. I No. 2 (New Orleans April, 1915).
—- Vol. I No. 3 (New Orleans May, 1915).
—- Vol. I No. 7 (New Orleans January, 1916).
—- Vol. I No. 9 (New Orleans March, 1916).
—- Vol. I No. 12 (New Orleans June, 1916).
Silent Defense, The: A Story of the Remarkable Trial of Members of the Industrial Workers of the World Held at Sacramento, California (Industrial Workers of the World: Chicago, 1918).
Voice of the People 28 Vol. II No. 28 (New Orleans July 17th, 1913).
—- [29] Vol. II No. 29 (New Orleans July 24th, 1913).
—- [30] Vol. II No. 30 (New Orleans July 31st, 1913).
—- [31] Vol. II No. 31 (New Orleans August 7th, 1913).
—- [32] Vol. II No. 32 (New Orleans August 14th, 1913).
—- [33] Vol. II No. 33 (New Orleans August 21st, 1913).
—- [34] Vol. II No. 34 (New Orleans August 28th, 1913).
—- [35] Vol. II No. 35 (New Orleans September 4th, 1913).
—- [36] Vol. II No. 36 (New Orleans September 11th, 1913).
—- [37] Vol. II No. 37 (New Orleans September 18th, 1913).
—- [38] Vol. II No. 38 (New Orleans September 25th, 1913).
—- [39] Vol. II No. 39 (New Orleans October 2nd, 1913).
—- [40] Vol. II No. 40 (New Orleans October 9th, 1913).
—- [41] Vol. II No. 41 (New Orleans October 16th, 1913).
—- [42] Vol. II No. 42 (New Orleans October 23rd, 1913).
—- [43] Vol. II No. 43 (New Orleans October 30th, 1913).
—- [44] Vol. II No. 44 (New Orleans November 6th, 1913).
—- [45] Vol. II No. 45 (New Orleans November 13th, 1913).
—- [46] Vol. II No. 46 (New Orleans November 20th, 1913).
—- [47] Vol. II No. 47 (New Orleans November 27th, 1913).
—- 48 Vol. II No. 48 (New Orleans December 4th, 1913).
—- 49 Vol. II No. 49 (New Orleans December 11th, 1913).
—- 50 Vol. II No. 50 (New Orleans December 18th, 1913).
—- 51 Vol. II No. 51 (New Orleans December 25th, 1913).
—- 52 Vol. III No. 1 (New Orleans January 1st, 1914).
—- 53 Vol. III No. 2 (New Orleans January 8th, 1914).
—- 54 Vol. III No. 3 (New Orleans January 15th, 1914).
—- 55 Vol. III No. 4 (New Orleans January 22nd, 1914).
—- 56 Vol. III No. 5 (New Orleans January 29th, 1914).
—- 57 Vol. III No. 6 (New Orleans February 5th, 1914).
—- 58 Vol. III No. 7 (New Orleans February 12th, 1914).
—- 59 Vol. III No. 8 (New Orleans February 19th, 1914).
—- 60 Vol. III No. 9 (New Orleans February 26th, 1914).
—- 61 Vol. III No. 10 (New Orleans March 5th, 1914).

—- 62 Vol. III No. 11 (New Orleans March 12th, 1914).
—- 63 Vol. III No. 12 (New Orleans March 19th, 1914).
—- 64 Vol. III No. 13 (New Orleans March 26th, 1914).
—- 65 Vol. III No. 14 (New Orleans April 2nd, 1914).
—- 66 Vol. III No. 15 (New Orleans April 9th, 1914).
—- 67 Vol. III No. 16 (New Orleans April 16th, 1914).
—- 68 Vol. III No. 17 (New Orleans April 23rd, 1914).
—- 69 Vol. III No. 18 (New Orleans May 1st, 1914).
—- 70 Vol. III No. 19 (New Orleans May 7th, 1914).
—- 71 Vol. III No. 20 (New Orleans May 14th, 1914).
—- 72 Vol. III No. 21 (New Orleans May 21st, 1914).
—- 73 Vol. III No. 22 (New Orleans May 28th, 1914).
—- 74 Vol. III No. 23 (New Orleans June 4th, 1914).
—- 75 Vol. III No. 24 (New Orleans June 11th, 1914).
—- 76 Vol. III No. 25 (New Orleans June 18th, 1914).
—- 77 Vol. III No. 26 (New Orleans June 30, 1914).
—- 78 Vol. III No. 27 (New Orleans July 7th, 1914).
—- 79 Vol. III No. 27 [sic] (New Orleans July 14th, 1914).
—- 80 Vol. III No. 28 (New Orleans July 21st, 1914).
—- 81 Vol. III No. 29 (Portland July 30th, 1914).
—- 82 Vol. III No. 30 (Portland August 6th, 1914).
—- 83 Vol. III No. 31 (Portland August 13th, 1914).
—- 84 Vol. III No. 32 (Portland August 20th, 1914).
—- 85 Vol. III No. 33 (Portland August 27th, 1914).
—- 86 Vol. II No. 34 (Portland September 3rd, 1914).
—- 87 Vol. II No. 35 (Portland September 10th, 1914).
—- 88 Vol. II No. 36 (Portland September 17th, 1914).
—- 89 Vol. II No. 37 (Portland October 1st, 1914).
—- 90 Vol. II No. 38 (Portland October 8th, 1914).
—- 91 Vol. II No. 39 (Portland October 15th, 1914).
—- 92 Vol. II No. 40 (Portland October 22th, 1914).
—- 93 Vol. II No. 41 (Portland October 29th, 1914).
—- 94 Vol. II No. 42 (Portland November 5th, 1914).
—- 95 Vol. II No. 43 (Portland November 12th, 1914).
—- 96 Vol. II No. 44 (Portland November 19th, 1914).
—- 97 Vol. II No. 45 (Portland November 26th, 1914).

"Might is Right" Cartoon
Punch (1853)

MIGHT IS RIGHT.

Van Driver. "I DON'T KNOW NUTHUN ABOUT NO RIGHT SIDES NOR WRONG SIDES. YOU GET OUT OF THE WAY, IF YER DON'T WANT TO BE MADE A WAFER OF!"

(Where are the Police?)

Ragnar Redbeard in the *Berkeley Barb*
Trevor Blake   (2019)

The *Berkeley Barb* (1965–1980) was an underground newspaper published in Berkeley California. While this classified advertisement mentioning Ragnar Redbeard is in itself trivial, it is significant in that it appears at a time when Redbeard and his work were out of print and out of favor. From the March 28th–April 3rd and April 4th–10th issues of the *Berkeley Barb* in 1969.

> CAN GOD BE TRUSSED?
>
> RAGNAR REDBEARD COME HOME; MIGHT IS RIGHT! UNFORTUNATELY, the Lord said not, which cheek to turn, and thus begat both charity and sodomy.

Three from *Reedy's Mirror*
(Various) (1917)

Reedy's Mirror Volume XXVI Number 12 St. Louis
(Friday March 23rd, 1917) page 196.

Who is Ragnar Redbeard?
Creston, Ia, March 15, 1917.
Editor of Reedy's Mirror:

Who was or is Ragnar Redbeard? He is the author of a remarkable book, "Might is Right," printed in Chicago about 1895 or 96. His name on the title page is followed by "LL.D., University of C—."

The book is the first and the bluntest expression in this country of the doctrine or dogma now designated Nietzcheism. It is well though brutally written and atrociously printed. It declares for no God, no charity, no sympathy. The weakest must go to the wall. The masses are the rabble. For everything we call Christian there is contempt and disgust. The Saviour is a Jewish slave, and so forth.

Issued in the year of the rise of Bryan's star, contemporaneously with "Coin's Financial School," this book *might* be a piece of gigantic irony; but it is too intense for that. Ragnar Redbeard is said in a preface to be the owner of a large ranch in Montana. The writing of the man is quite tremendous. He knew something, but, he says, not much of Nietzsche, Felix Dahn and others. The book, he says, was begun in 1890 before he knew anything about them.

I have made inquiries concerning him in Chicago, where the book was published. I have not been able to learn anything about him. Some old-time anarchists say they think he is dead.

The book, for all its rawness, deserves a place alongside Winwood Reade's "The Martyrdom of Man." I find that there was an English edition, maybe two or three, the latest in 1910. Ragnar Redbeard is evidently a pen-name. He is quoted and advertised in *The Eagle and the Serpent*, the first English periodical, at first a weekly, then a monthly, devoted to the Nietzschean propaganda. The periodical published as news large excerpts from Prof. Thomas Commons' translation of "Thus Spake Zarathustra."

The editor of the MIRROR seems to have a way of finding out things and possibly he can uncover for me the identity of the man who was the first exponent of Nietzscheanism in all its naked thing-in-itselfness.

MACKEY-STIRNER.

[The editor's copy of "Might is Right" shows the book was entered according to the act of congress in 1897, by Arthur Uing. It has for secondary title, "The Gospel of Chicago." It is of a fifth edition of 10,000, published by W. J. Robbins & Co., Ltd. 20 Midhope Abbey, Cromer St., Gray's Inn Road, 1910. It contains an editor's preface to the 1896 edition, signed "Douglas K. Handyside, M. D., Ph. D." A preface to the 6th edition, 1903, conveys the information that "the author (who owns a cattle ranch in Montana of 30,000 acres) refuses to revise, correct or make any alterations in the text." Dr. Redbeard is described as "a literal reincarnation of Wodin." The book is said to have inspired "Col. Roosevelt's gospel of Roman strenuousness." Cecil Rhodes is said to have had his own private copy typewritten for better convenience and study. It is the worst-printed book in the world. It is to be had now of Thurland and Thurland, Evanston, Ill.]

Editor of the MIRROR.

∉

Reedy's Mirror Volume XXVI Number 13 St. Louis
(Friday March 30th 1917) page 220:

Ragnar Redbeard in Rhyme

St. Louis, March 24, 1917.

Editor of Reedy's Mirror:

Have just read the letter in your issue of March 23, and your note thereupon, about Ragnar Redbeard, LL.D. I have a copy of "Might is Right" and I think it is a remarkable presentation of the "last word" of the evolutionary philosophy. Ragnar Redbeard does not gloss the brutal truth, does not sugar the pill. And all altruism to the contrary, it is the truth. It does, as your correspondent says, reiterate the dogma of Winwood Reade, brother of him who wrote "The Cloister and the Hearth," that "the human soul must die," as uttered in the last chapter of "The Martyrdom of Man"—a truth that was maintained well by Francis Newman, the strange brother of Cardinal John Henry Newman of the "Grammar of Assent" and the "Apoligia pro Vita Sua." You might give your readers the essence of Ragnar Redbeard's philosophy by reprinting the poem with which "Might is Right" is concluded—"The Logic of To-Day." The sub-title of Redbeard's volume is an inspiration—"The Gospel of Chicago." It is interesting to contrast the fulminations of the prophet of Chicago with those of "the prophet of San Francisco"—Henry George.

Rousseau Jones.

THE LOGIC OF TO-DAY

"Inferior organisms succumb and perish or are enslaved. Superior organisms survive, propagate and POSSESS." —Darwin.

"All men are created equal" —is an infernal lie.

"Not by speechifying and majority votes can the great questions of To-Day be settled . . . but by iron and blood."—Bismarck.

> Might was right when Caesar bled
>   Upon the stones of Rome,
> Might was Right when Joshua led
>   His hordes o'er Jordan's foam,
> And Might was Right when German troops
>   Poured down through Paris gay;
> It's the Gospel of the Ancient World
>   And the Logic of To-day.
>
> Behind all Kings and Presidents
>   All Government and Law,
> Are army-corps and cannoneers
>   To hold the world in awe.
> And sword-strong races own the earth
>   And ride the Conqueror's Car,
> And *Liberty* has never been won,
>   Except by deeds of war.
>
> What are the lords of hoarded gold—
>   The silent Semite rings?
> What are the plunder-patriots—
>   High-pontiffs, priests and kings?
> What are they but bold master-minds,

Best fitted for the fray?
Who comprehend and vanquish by
    The Logic of To-day?

Cain's knotted club is scepter still—
    The "Rights of Man" is fraud:
Christ's Ethics are for creeping things—
    True manhood smiles at "God."
For Might is Right when empires sink
    In storms of steel and flame;
And it is *Right* when weakling breeds
    Are hunted down like game.

Then what's the use of dreaming dreams—
    That "each shall get his own"
By forceless votes of meek-eyed thralls,
    Who blindly sweat and moan?
No! A curse is on their cankered brains—
    Their very bones decay:
Go! trace your fate in the Iron Game,
    Is the Logic of To-day.

The Strong must ever rule the Weak,
    Is grim Primordial Law—
On earth's broad racial threshing floor,
    The Meek are beaten straw.
Then ride to Power o'er foemens neck
    Let *nothing* bar your way,
If you are *fit* you'll rule and reign,
    Is the Logic of To-day.

You must prove your Right by deeds of Might—
    Of splendor and renown.
If need-be march through flames of hell,
    To dash opponents down—
If need-be die on scaffold high
    In the mornings misty gray
For "Liberty or Death" is still
    The Logic of To-day.

Might was Right when Gideon led
    The "chosen" tribes of old,
And it was right when Titus burnt
    Their Temple roofed with gold:
And Might was Right from Bunker Hill
    To far Manilla Bay,
By land and flood it's wrote in blood—
    The Gospel of To-day.

"Put no trust in princes"
    Is a saying old and true,
"Put no hope in Governments"
    Translateth it anew.
All "Books of Law" and "Golden Rules"
    Are fashioned to betray;
"The Survival of the Strongest"
    Is the Gospel of To-day.

Might was Right when Carthage flames,
    Lit up the Punic foam,
And—when the naked steel of Gaul,
    Weighed down the spoil of Rome;
And Might was Right when Richmond fell—
    And at Thermopylae—
It's the Logic of the Ancient World
    And the Gospel of To-day.

Where pendant suns in millions swing,
    Around this whirling earth,
It's Might, it's Force that holds the brakes,
    And steers through life and death:
Force governs all organic life,
    Inspires all Right and Wrong.
It's Nature's plan to weed-out man,
    And test who are the Strong.

∉

Reedy's Mirror Volume XXVI Number 15 St. Louis
(Friday April 13Th 1917) Page 260

"Ragnar Redbeard" a St. Louisan?

New York, April 3, 1917.

Editor of Reedy's Mirror:

I notice in the March 23rd and 30th issues the letters from Mackey Stirner and Rousseau Jones—both pen names evidently—concerning "Might is Right," by Ragnar Redbeard.

In 1905, N. P. L. Rosch, now deceased, gave to me the proof sheets of "Might is Right" to read, stating he was the author and that the book would be printed by some publishing concern in Chicago and requested me to make no mention of his being the author.

Mr. Rosch subscribed literally to the doctrine that "Right is Might" and many is the argument I have had with him concerning that subject.

OSCAR AURELIUS MORGNER.

[Nicholas P. L. Rosch read to the editor of the MIRROR about 1905 what was probably the "proof" referred to by O. A. M. It was a ferocious assault upon Democracy, Christianity, charity, virtue, and all the accepted sanctities. On first reading "Might is Right," the editor suspected Rosch, but lacked evidence. He does not now recall that Rosch's booklet in proof bore the title "Might is Right," but Rosch may very well have been "Ragnar Redbeard." He did not want the substance of the proofs he passed around made generally known.

Rosch was at one time associated in the practice of law with John Peter Altgeld, in Chicago. He came to St. Louis about 1905 and first gained some local distinction in a small way as an attorney for some of the followers of the late state Senator Tom Kinney. He organized a Democratic club in the brewery region and not proving tractable to the political bosses his club was broken up and he was slugged. He published broadsides attacking Democratic politicians and distributed them at conventions. He had talent as a rough-and-ready caricaturist as well as a vituperative writer. He took up the cause of prohibition and wrote and drew for it, violently. Once he ran for the Democratic nomination for Circuit Attorney on a campaign fund of about nine dollars. Later he went to Venice, Ills., and started a paper called *The Gondola*, that lasted about three weeks. It was too hot for Venice. Rosch died somewhat more than a year ago—having returned to the fold from which he had strayed—Roman Catholicism.

Messrs. Thurland and Thurland, publishers of "Might is Right," Evanston, Ills., are inclined to doubt Mr. Rosch's authorship. Mr. Rosch was a customer of theirs away back in the '90s. He received copies of the book from the earliest edition imported from England. He ordered a copy once to be sent to Tom Watson of Georgia. It had a notable effect on Watson. Governor Altgeld once quoted from the book in an oration against government by judges, but the newspapers suppressed the quotation. Messrs. Thurland and Thurland give some history of the book:

"The first publisher in London was named Bowman or Bowerman and the book was sold by Foyle, Charing Cross Road, and by Simpkins Marshall. In Chicago it was brought out at first by Mueller & Co., Garden City Block. This firm bankrupted about 1900. The University of Chicago wrote us some years ago as to the personality of the author, who was said to have been a teacher there for two years. Prof. Von Otto Ammon of Berlin translated "Might is Right" into German, eighteen years ago, in condensed form. The first copies of the book were typewritten and stitched together with wire and bound in cloth. Perhaps Mr. Rosch had one of these. We are inclined to think the style in which the book is printed is in the nature of a disguise—the author apparently did not want to be known. Bernard Shaw once said the book would produce a thousand revolutions yet."]

Commentary on Redbeard in *Reedy's Mirror*
Trevor Blake (2019)

The man who wrote as Ragnar Redbeard generally declined to sign his name of birth to his creation. The secret identity of this literal reincarnation of Wodin was known in his antipodean home, but did not survive his arrival in Chicago. Within twenty years of publication, the author of *Might is Right* had disappeared behind his pseudonym. Even the intent of *Might is Right* (was it irony or philosophy?) began to blur. By 1917 Chicago was lousy with members of the Industrial Workers of the World, among them anarchists and enthusiasts for Ragnar Redbeard. It seems even they did not know Redbeard walked those same streets.

Some of these authors are unknown. For instance, who was "Mackay-Stirner" of Creston, Indiana? John Henry Mackay (1864–1933) was the author of *Max Stirner: sein Leben und sein Werk* (1898, 1910, 1914) and this is the sure reference of the writer. In 1917 Mackay was in Berlin and Stirner had no more Leben left, so the identity of the Indiana egoist, like Rousseau Jones, remains unknown.

Redbeard said he knew something but not much of Friedrich Nietzsche (1844–1900), Felix Dahn (1834–1912) in *Might is Right* (AMiR A.3:9). *Might is Right* was not the first expression of Nietzcheism in the United States. That honor goes to *The Works of Nietzsche* translated by Thomas Common (New York: The Macmillan Company, 1896) (AMiR A.3:9). The star of William Jennings Bryan (1860–1925) rose in 1896 but did not shine bright enough to win the office of President of the United States. William Hope Harvey (1851–1936) was an aid to Bryan's campaign. Harvey was also the author of "Coin's Financial School," an appeal for the return of bimetalism.

Bimetalism! The United States has been on a no-metal-ism financial basis for enough generations that it is difficult to understand how worked up some men were about the issue of a gold standard for money versus a dual gold and silver standard. Also difficult to understand today is the global rage for and against the economic writings of Henry George 1839–1897) (AMiR 2.7:2). Winwood Reade (1838–1875) appears in *Might is Right* (AMiR 6.6:9) in an allusion to his *Matyrdom of Man* (London: Kegan, Paul, Trench & Truber, 1872). Reade's writing was significant enough to be essential to Charles Darwin's *The Descent of Man* but is not widely known today. Reade's brother Charles (1814–1884) wrote "The Cloister and the Hearth," many times more popular than *Martyrdom of Man* in its day and therefore all the more neglected now. Cardinal John Henry Newman (1801–1890) was known for his autobiography *Apologia Pro Vita Sua* (London: 1865) and his book of theology *An Essay in Aid of a Grammar of Assent* (London: Longmans, Green and Co., 1870). His younger brother Francis William Newman (1805–1897) was also an author. The Brothers Reade and Newman are stars that have dimmed. I like to learn about the debates that swamped the planet in the past which are forgotten now, because it offers a point of perspective for the debates that swamp the planet today. Or are the hot topics of today super-duper real and important, to be resolved or at least remembered forever?

There was an English edition of *Might is Right* and it was published in 1910. Before *Might is Right* Redbeard released a series of booklets that collectively were called "Redbeard's Reader." One of the Readers, *Women and War*, was folded into *Might is Right*. *Might is Right* was advertised in *The Eagle and The Serpent*. Redbeard served as the editor of same for an issue. It was among the earliest English-language publishers of Nietzsche (and Stirner, and Redbeard, and Malfew Seklew...). The address of the UK publisher and the physical description of the wire-bound manuscript are found nowhere else.

The Torah, or the Pentateuch (the first five books of the Christian Bible), is traditionally ascribed to Moses. Which is another one of G_d's miracles because these books describe the life of Moses, and his death, and continue on from there. Similarly, Cecil Rhodes is said to have been an enthusiast of *Might is Right* and he was mentioned favorably in *Might is Right*. Which came first? It is true that Redbeard claimed the acclaim of Rhodes, but did Rhodes dote on Redbeard?

Nicholas P. L. Rosch was an investor in the Thomure-Gebhard Custom Shirt Company of St. Louis, according to *Men's Wear* (Chicago: July 8th, 1908. Vol. XXV No. V Page 58). *Gould's St. Louis Directory* for 1920 lists Rosch as the President of same (page 2843). Rosch was described as an agitator for the Bryan-Hadley Club by the *Kansas City Times* (August 27th, 1908), indicating his support for Presidential candidate Bryan. An agitator he may have been, for he suffered a wound to his head from roughs who broke up a Bryan meeting (*St. Louis Post-Dispatch* June 6th, 1908).

He ran for Circuit Attorney in St. Louis for that year (*St. Louis Post-Dispatch* November 10th, 1908). The *St. Louis Post-Dispatch* listed him as an investigator of campaign tax-dodgers (March 20th, 1909). Said investigation went to trial (*St. Louis Star and Times* July 11th, 1910) and while Rosch may have been an attorney, he was not known to show up to court (*St. Louis Post-Dispatch* March 25th, 1909). Eventually he withdrew from the case (*St. Louis Post-Dispatch* February 14th, 1911). But... was he a client of Thurland & Thurland, publishers and distributors of *Might is Right*? Did he claim to be the author of *Might is Right*? A claim no more ridiculous than that the author of the "Gospel of Chicago" was an ice-cream salesman, but one with less evidence.

ARTHUR DESMOND SATIRIZED
(NEW ZEALAND OBSERVER) (1890)

THE DESMOND CHARGES; OR, THE SADDLE ON THE WRONG HORSE.

DESMOND (putting saddle on Zealandia)—'I shall mount this horse—a gallant Grey—and he will carry me to victory.'
ADAM KELLY (watching his movements)—'You're in Van Douse(n) of a hurry to fix that saddle. Perhaps somebody may want to ride the other horse, which has the best claim to it.'

HOUSE OF GOWRIE ADVERTISEMENT
ARTHUR DESMOND (N.D.)

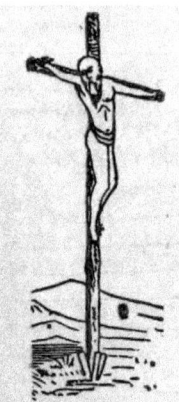

REMEMBER!

If you want a book of any kind, write to me. If I have not got it, I know where to find it (if it is in print). Don't always expect an immediate reply, however. Give me time to find out, and when I've something definite to say, be sure I'll say it.

THE FIRST ANARCHIST

BY
VICTOR HUGO.

Author of Les Miserables, Notre Dame, Hans of Iceland, Napoleon the Little etc. etc.

"THEY"

They cast me into prison with lash and curse and blow: they bruised my face with bludgeons, and spat upon my brow.
They haled me to the judgement, with frenzied oath and lie: and called me "malefactor" and said that I must die.
They spiked me to a gallows, and stabbed me through the side; and crowned my head with briar, and mocked me as I died. I. H. S.

> The Son of God goes forth to war,
> A kingly crown to gain,
> His blood Red banner streams afar:
> Who follows in his train?
>   Authorised Episcopal Hymn. No 507.

The State! Whatever the State saith is a lie: whatever it hath is a theft: all is counterfeit in it: the gnawing, sanguinary, insatiate Monster. it even bites with stolen teeth --- it's very Bowels are counterfeit." NIETZSCHE.

PRICE 5c.
THE HOUSE OF GOWRIE
Importers — Publishers — Printers — Booksellers
364 Wendell St.   Chicago, Ill.

Patrons, a Gratitude
Kevin I. Slaughter & Trevor Blake

Special thanks to our patrons at Patreon. By socializing their selfishness, they have allowed us to acquire some of the egoist treasures that make up *Der Geist* and UnionOfEgoists.com. See the address below for details on the rich rewards returned to those who make even the most comfortable of contributions to our cause. The patrons below supported us between November 2018 and November 2019.

Raul A.
Luigi Santos-Hammarlund
Robert Carmonius
Louis Perrotta
Matt Godwin
George Lightfoot
Logospilgrim
Neil Alvarado
Richard P. Smith
The Independent Ego
Jim Jesus
Waylon Strobehn
Max Hill
Thomas H. Moreland
Eric Rowe
S
JP
Dustin Newman
Eugene Plawiuk
Richard
Johnny Beach Vota
Dayan Weller
Wes
The Accusation Network
METASKILLS
Jacob Kirkland
Alexandria
Asura
Brandon Matthews
Stephen
Frank Plissken
Joachim Kulla
Jeff Bowling
Justin Thomas
Curtis Taylor Price
Robert Cueva Jr
Brian Lamay
Robert Sherwood

WWW.PATREON.COM/UNIONOFEGOISTS

About the Editors

Kevin I. Slaughter (b. 1975) is a graphic designer and book publisher by vocation and intellectual dissident and misanthropologist by avocation.

He is the Archivist for the Sidney E. Parker Archives (sidparker.com) and the Benjamin DeCasseres website (benjamindecasseres.com), is the editor for the egoist journal *Stand Alone*, and in 2012 edited *A Bible not Borrowed from the Neighbors: Essays and Aphorisms on Egoism*. In 2019 he published *Might is Right: The Authoritative Edition*, the first in a series of Redbeard books.

He has lectured at Universities on the topic of Satanism, and an hour long presentation titled "Satanism as Weltanschauung: The Philosophy of the Church of Satan" is available on YouTube. He has won the Robert G. Ingersoll Oratory Award.

He admires the outsider genius, the architects of their own worlds—opinions be damned. He is uncomfortable with false dichotomies, understands that however rational he tries to be his consciousness is controlled in part by genetically borne biases and his understanding of the world is skewed by the poor construction of biology that nature has evolved. He's more and more inclined to believe nobody is right, but he's less wrong than most.

Trevor Blake (b. 1966) is the author of *Confessions of a Failed Egoist*, *Max Stirner Bibliography* and *The Eagle and the Serpent Index of Names*. He has written introductions to reprinted books by egoists including *The Gospel of Malfew Seklew* by Malfew Seklew, *For Love and Money* by Leighton Pagan, *The Martyrdom of Percy Whitcomb* by Erwin McCall, and *The Philosophy of Time* by Dora Marsden. Trevor has published 1.2 million words of the British philosopher George Walford at gwiep.net, and *Buckminster Fuller Bibliography* at synchronofile.com. Since 1987 he has published the magazine OVO, details of which are at ovo127.com. He lives in Portland, Oregon.

www.ingramcontent.com/pod-product-compliance
Lightning Source LLC
Chambersburg PA
CBHW071204090426
42736CB00030B/2858